The Joys of Aging—

and how to avoid them

Also by Phyllis Diller:

PHYLLIS DILLER'S HOUSEKEEPING HINTS

PHYLLIS DILLER'S MARRIAGE MANUAL

THE COMPLETE MOTHER

The Joys of Aging—
and how to avoid them

Can sex keep you young?
and other silly questions
thoroughly demolished
by

PHYLLIS DILLER

Illustrated by NORMAN KLEIN

Doubleday & Company, Inc.
Garden City, New York
1981

Library of Congress Cataloging in Publication Data

Diller, Phyllis.
The Joys of Aging—and How to Avoid Them.

1. Aging—Anecdotes, facetiae, satire, etc.
I. Title.
PN6231.A43D5   818'.5402
ISBN: 0-385-14555-1
Library of Congress Catalog Card Number 79–7863

First Edition

BOOK DESIGN BY BENTE HAMANN

Phyllis Diller wishes to thank Arnie Kogen for his contribution to the text of this book.

Contents

Foreword

This book is a primer on how to look and stay young. You may be asking yourself, "Why is Phyllis Diller writing a book giving advice on staying young?" That's like Don Rickles writing a book on "Common Courtesy."

The fact is I've dedicated my life to staying young. It may not look it, but I have. In fact, I've worked so hard on staying young it's beginning to age me.

I've done EVERYTHING . . . I've gone to spas in Switzerland, taken hormone shots, had plastic surgery, cellulite treatments, vitamins, miracle drugs, miracle moisture cream, Miracle Whip. I've stolen some cells from Dick Clark's body and transplanted them into mine. It didn't work. I started to grow facial hair and in the middle of the night I found myself saying, "It's got a good beat but it's kinda hard to dance to."

This book will teach you not only how to look young and feel young, but give you inexpensive, practical ways to make old age work for you. If you can't afford to touch up your face, I'll show you how to "touch up" the date of birth on your driver's license. I'll teach you how to make varicose veins into an erogenous zone. Show you how to make stretch marks blend in with the current disco "swirl" fashions.

Yes, even though I chug-a-lug Geritol, I will show you how to become part of the Pepsi Generation.

If I can do it, you can do it.

The Joys of Aging—

and how to avoid them

1

Young Is Better Than Old

SOME ABSOLUTE TRUTHS:

Sir Laurence Olivier is a better dramatic actor than Soupy Sales.

Iceberg Lettuce is better for you than banana cream pie.

The sun is hotter than a Fudgsicle.

Wilt Chamberlain is taller than most William Morris agents.

and

YOUNG IS BETTER THAN OLD!

SOME AXIOMS:

Watergate was embarrassing to Nixon.

A kiss on the mouth from Burt Reynolds couldn't hurt you.

Mud wrestling is messier than stamp collecting.

A quick nap will do wonders for you . . . especially if it's with someone.

and

YOUNG IS BETTER THAN OLD!

I'm sure there are some people out there, some skeptics, some misguided loonies who think old is better than young. There are people who still cling to the outmoded theory that "life begins at 40" . . . you're not getting older, you're getting better. These are the same people who applauded the minting of the Susan B. Anthony dollar, and who chuckle at demolition derbies.

Sure, you may say there were some brilliant, vital old people. And there *were*. Albert Schweitzer was a great humanitarian, but could he get a date for New Year's Eve? Grandma Moses could paint the hell out of a landscape, but could she paint the town red? Let's face it—young is definitely better than old. Okay, now that that's settled, how do we stay young? How do we keep our youth? (I have one friend, Lenore, who keeps him in the guest closet.)

There are practical ways to stay young. We will get to these. Things like spas, clinics, diet, exercise, sex (look through the book for the "well-thumbed" pages). We can have ourselves tucked, pinched, pulled, snipped, surgically adjusted. Desperate people, like me, also turn to religion.

I once grabbed Charlton Heston at a party. I begged, "You've got the power. Please . . . do something for me!"

Right there he turned to his wife and composed the Eleventh Commandment. "Thou shalt not attend parties with Phyllis Diller." He parted the Perrier waters on the buffet table and made his way out the door. I have prayed to the Norse God of Youth, Preyja, to remove my stretch marks. I pray to the Norse Gods often. I have also prayed to "Shecky"—The Norse God of Stand-up Comedians—for new material. He said, "Are you the lady with the stretch marks? If you are, forget it!"

IF THERE'S A FOUNTAIN OF YOUTH, WILL I NEED A SNORKEL?

I was in Florida recently working one of the big hotels. The crowd was mostly retired senior citizens. I was a smash . . . They loved me! Ever notice how Tom Jones's fans throw their room keys up on stage? These people were tossing Polident! They applauded by slapping their Social Security cards together. It was the first time I ever got a "crouching ovation." A stunned realization hit me along with a Wendell Willkie button . . . half these people are younger than I am!

When I got off stage and into my dressing room I turned to my agent. "It's gotta be around here somewhere."
    "What? . . . your makeup remover kit with the trowel?"
    "No, the Fountain of Youth. Ponce de León searched for it here in Florida. Tomorrow I'm going out looking for it."
    "You're crazy!" he scoffed. "It's a silly legend."

"I'm going," I insisted, "and I'm coming back younger! I'm packing a lunch of pablum, mother's milk, and Gerber's apple sauce."

His parting words to me were, "If you find it, I get ten percent of it."

The next morning I was on a chartered boat chugging through the Everglades. I was searching for the Fountain of Youth. What would it look like? I wasn't quite sure. I kept squinting along the shore looking for a body of water where the lifeguards were only three years old.

Wouldn't it be great if Ponce de León fountain truly did exist? Imagine . . . you'd step in the water as old Aunt Agatha and you'd come out as Brooke Shields! The DAR would go in and they'd come out as the Dallas Cowboys Cheerleaders! Just my luck—if I found the Fountain of Youth, Jaws would be swimming around in it. What if I just went in up to my toes? . . . Would I end up with young *feet?*

I finally ended my search in Florida's Disney World. I wondered . . . is this the Fountain of Youth? Then realized it *had* to be. After all, Mickey Mouse is fifty years old . . . He still looks twelve.

ONE PICTURE OF DORIAN GRAY
IS WORTH A THOUSAND FACE-LIFTS

The Picture of Dorian Gray was one of three classic motion pictures that have changed the course of my life. The other two were *Keep 'Em Slugging,* with Huntz Hall, and *The Three Stooges Have Trouble Churning Whipped Cream.*

If you remember (those of us over forty do, those of us under forty are too busy with other things to even care), Dorian Gray is a man who sells his soul in exchange for eternal youth. He continues to stay young while his portrait keeps getting older and older. You may be saying to yourselves: would Phyllis Diller sell her soul to be younger? ARE YOU KIDDING?!! Would Farrah Fawcett endorse shampoo? Would Dean Martin say yes to a martini? Would Ronald Reagan pop jelly beans?

I would do *anything* to be younger. I would certainly go for a deal like Dorian Gray and let my picture become older. However, this could be disastrous for any house that picture is hanging in. Do you know how quickly property values would plummet? There'd be more cracks in that canvas than at a Friars' roast for the Ayatollah Khomeini. Picasso painted a picture with one eye. This one would probably end up having four chins and seven necks. The only public place they could hang my picture would be The Museum of Cardiac Arrest.

Alas, as much as we may search, hope, and dream, unfortunately there is no Fountain of Youth and no magic paint-

ings that will grow older while we stay young. There are no miracles to stop the aging process. I even tried going in a Time Machine. It was a cheap, unsophisticated model constructed by my neighbor's son as a science project. I went inside, pulled the lever and went back twenty-four hours. I had to sit through Howard Cosell twice that week.

There are no magic formulas for getting younger. Only hard work and the right psychological attitude will do it. You have to start to think young, talk young, act young. Learn to go with the flow. Get rid of and replace everything that even suggests "old." Here are some suggestions:

· Hide that enema bag and replace it with a pulsating shower massage!

· Melt down all your *Naughty Marietta* albums!

· Burn all your doilies!

· Don't ever say the words "Girdle," "Bobby Sox," or "Fred Waring."

· Say things like, "Oh, wow," "All Righhhhht," "I can relate to your karma," and, "I've got something heavy to lay on you," even if you don't know what they mean.

· Get a face-lift!

If you don't have this last one, the others will help you about as much as a training bra on Dolly Parton. Read on!

2

Face-lifts: Medicine's Way of Telling Nature to Flake Off! (And Other Cosmetic Surgery Procedures)

Thanks to cosmetic surgery, "Sorry, I was born this way" is no longer a valid excuse for looking like something the cat dragged in. If your nose is too big, your eyes too baggy, your chins too many, cosmetic surgery can do wonders for you.

A face-lift can make you look years younger and can enhance that battered self image. However, not everyone needs a face-lift. You need a face-lift if:

- Your face is sagging faster than the American dollar.

- You occasionally trip over your neck.

• Parker Brothers wants to market your face as a new party game for children.

• A family of Gypsies has set up house in one of your face crevices.

• Philosophers have used your face as proof that there is no God.

SHOPPING AROUND FOR "DR. RIGHT"

A little historical background.

The first face-lift was performed in Kiev in 1836 by Boris Bladsky, a Russian tailor, on his wife, Rimska, who had very bad jowls and was constantly depressed about it. Using no anesthesia and a primitive sewing machine, Bladsky not only successfully "took in" his wife's face, but made cuffs out of the excess.

We've come a long way since Boris. (By the way, the legend continues: his wife looked so sensational after the face-lift that she eventually ran away with Tevya, a handsome silo foreman on a Minsk farfel farm.) Now, in the 1980s, surgical techniques have become much more sophisticated. However, it is still *your* face we're talking about. You are literally putting it in someone's hands. If you do decide to have your face "done," you should select a surgeon very carefully. The right doctor can slow down the hands of time. The wrong doctor might make your face look like it's been through a Timex Torture Test.

There are many excellent cosmetic surgeons around, but there are also quite a few quacks. Fortunately, there is a plastic surgeons' union which oversees the conduct of its members. Unfortunately, they call themselves, "Facial and Reconstructive Cosmetic Engineers." This spells out FARCE.

In selecting a surgeon you must use your own judgment and instincts. From vast experience I can offer some guidelines.

Be suspicious of any plastic surgeon if:

• The diploma on his wall is from the "Whammo School of Medicine."

• More than three of his former patients now go by the nickname "Scarface."

• His office is located in the back of a Ford Econoline van . . . and it's moving!

• The word "Mattel" appears on the back of all his surgical equipment.

• A number of his patients were referred to him by a Dr Joseph Mengele.

• His coin purse looks like someone you know.

PICKING YOUR FACE

I've had virtually every cosmetic surgical procedure there is, and thanks to President Truman, I didn't have to pay a cent for it! (Back in 1951, he declared my body a disaster area, thus qualifying me for federal funds.)

DIPLOMA
WHAMMO
SCHOOL
OF
MEDICINE

DR SUESS

For those of you who aren't fortunate enough to have their bodies federally funded, the face-lift will be expensive, but it will be worth it.

Of course fees will vary depending on the face you select. Beware! Some cosmetic surgeons are crass, commercial opportunists who will try to capitalize on popular personalities. Many plastic surgeons will show you a chart of well-known beauties and ask you who you'd like to look like after surgery. A typical chart might look like this:

#222:	The Cheryl Ladd	$3,500
# 18:	The Candice Bergen	$3,250
#109:	The Elizabeth Taylor (Pre 1966)	$3,000
#396:	The Rula Lenska	$ 850
# 71:	The Wolfman Jack	$ 215

This week's special:

#422:	The Dolly Madison (as she looks *today*)	$ 29.99

I had fantasies like everyone else. I told my surgeon, Dr. Franklin Ashley, "I want to look like Raquel Welch . . . *after* she's had a good night's rest."

He was very direct and honest. "Phyllis, we are surgeons, not miracle workers. You cannot look like someone else. You can only look like a better version of *you*."

I said, "That's like telling the captain of the *Poseidon*, 'When your ship turns over it will only *partially* leak!'"

TV IS ALWAYS LOOKING FOR NEW FACES . . . I THOUGHT I'D GIVE THEM ONE

It's not easy to remember the exact moment I decided to have a face-lift.

Was it when I was twelve years old and woke up every morning and said, "Mirror, mirror on the wall . . . I don't want to hear it"?

Was it when I went to New York and asked for a part-time job in a department store and they made me a guard dog at Saks?

Was it when I went to unload my troubles to a psychiatrist and he said, "You're crazy!" I said, "I'd like another opinion." He said, "Okay, you're also ugly!"

All I know is I was made for plastic surgery the way Frisbees were made for flying. You've heard of the expression "face value"? I was in debt! I wanted to look younger and better, and I was willing to go through any pain and discomfort to achieve this.

My first face-lift was not a thrilling experience.

I checked into Earl Sheib General Hospital, 8:30 in the evening. Exactly 6 A.M. the next morning I was being wheeled into the Cosmetic Surgery Wing. That was the official name. Most patients called it "The Tuck Tower."

I was strapped on the operating table when the surgical team came in. I'll never forget their expressions as they glared down at me. They looked at my face the way a leading architectural planner looks at downtown Tijuana. It was not a sight they were pleased with. They called for their instruments . . . scalpel, suture, clamps, silly putty, crazy glue, Black & Decker power tools.

I was getting worried. The tension was building. Could they do it? Could they actually change the contours of my face? Hey, nothing to worry about. After all, these were doctors. Golfers. They had played sand traps before. One of them tried to lighten the moment and suggested playing "Connect-a-dot" with the liver spots on my face. I started worrying. Were they *really* good? When they went to Plastic Surgery School, did they all get "As" in *face*? Maybe one of them majored in "feet."

I started feeling the pressure. Certain little things were beginning to bother me.

Why did they put that sign over the entrance door, "Careful—Heavy Construction Going On"?

Why were all the young medical students observing in the gallery taking bets to 8-to-5 that the surgeon wouldn't get *all* the lines out?

Was the anesthesiologist really qualified? Why did he lean over to me and whisper, "You're in show business. What is Chuck Barris *really* like?"

PUT ON A PUFFY FACE

What's black and blue and red all over?

A)   A wounded blood clot

B)   An ink blot going through change of life

C)   The colors of a stupid rainbow

Ready? It's what your face looks like after cosmetic surgery. Yes, for the first few weeks you will be all puffy and swollen. You should have seen the post-face job ladies as we took our recuperative morning walk through the tuck tower. It looked like a reunion of battered wives. Black-eyed Susan is not the name of a flower, but a description of the lady in Room 412.

You feel terrible and awkward. Well-meaning friends and visitors don't help either. In an attempt to lighten the atmosphere they usually come in with gag gifts. My friend Cynthia brought me a jar to bring my old face home in. My Uncle Vernon, an ecology-minded recycling freak, wondered what they did with old skin after a face-lift. He suggested, "Perhaps they could send it to a needy person in a deprived country." Joan Rivers visited and said, "There's enough skin left over to make another person."

Of course a lot of women will never *admit* they had their faces "done." They won't let *anyone* see the scars and puffiness. They simply "disappear" for a few weeks in Acapulco while their faces settle. Others arrange their surgery so that the recuperative period takes place during a total eclipse.

I think the trick is to be creative. Openly walk around your neighborhood with your bruises showing and when friends ask why your face looks like a half a pound of ground round, tell them, "That's the last time I run a killer bee farm," or "I visited my Aunt Clara in Fresno, California, and there was an earthquake . . . from the neck up!"

THE UNVEILING

Some people are so proud of their face-lifts they like to throw "coming out" parties to show them off. I don't recommend it. I threw one of those parties and invited the press and show-business friends. The whole next day I was a nervous wreck waiting for the reviews to come in. My fears were well-founded. The reviews were mixed. Rex Reed called my face, "A disappointment. It sagged in places."

Some other reviews:

"A major structural achievement."
                                              UPI

"Uneven in spots. Needs tightening."
            ZACH, CLEVELAND DAILY NEWS

"A twisted masterpiece. Not since Hitchcock has anything been this shocking. Not for everyone. Children under seventeen should not be permitted to look without an adult in attendance."

                                    PEORIA JOURNAL

"I laughed at parts. I cried at others."
                    RONA BARRETT

"It lies there like so much dead fish."
            SASKATOON GAZETTE

AFTER THE FALL

Despite the mixed reviews I was thrilled with my facial surgery. A note of caution, however, about face-lifts. They are like displays in department store windows and John Derek's wives . . . they are not permanent! Like a shaky Central American dictatorship, it can fall when you least expect it.

This could happen in five to seven years, but beware . . . it could also happen sooner. Precautions should be taken. During the recuperative period it is very important to avoid sneezing, as this could cause your stitches to burst and your face to droop drastically. I strongly urge post-face-lift patients not to set up house in a field of goldenrod. Also to be avoided are roller-coaster rides, Brahma bull riding, biting into four-day-old bagels, and sex under the age of fifty-five. (If you're over fifty-five, don't worry. Nothing will break.)

To protect your friends and loved ones against unnecessary shock, I suggest you have a sign ready that says, "Caution—Falling Face."

A EUPHEMISM JOB

Besides face-lifts (rhytidectomy) there are many other sorts of reconstructive surgery available. The terms can get pretty confusing. I've compiled a glossary to help you out.

Familiar Name	Fancy Medical Name	Girl Talk—Slang Nickname
Nose job	Rhinoplasty	Beak overhaul or Schnoz snip
Having your eyes done	Blepharoplasty	Peeper keeper
Stomach flattening	Abdominal Lipectomy	Tummy tuck or Paunch pinch
Breast implant	Augmentation Mammaplasty	Boob job or Jug filler
Breast reduction	Reduction Mammaplasty	Boob bob or Tittie tuck
Buttock lift	Buttock Lipectomy	Bun upper
Ear job	Otoplasty	A dumbo do

A word about electrolysis. Electrolysis (nickname: fuzz flattener) has of course been around for years, and is a safe, painless way of permanently removing unwanted body hair. You can, however, get the same result much more cheaply simply by hanging around Harrisburg during a nuclear leak.

3

My Beauty and Skin-care Lecture at UCLA
(Or, "Take This Course and Get Absolutely No Credits")

I was invited recently by UCLA to lecture. Not on comedy, not on show business, not on cinema (although my most recent film, "Seven Brothers for One Bride—and They're Not Too Thrilled," received excellent reviews and I was quite compelling in the part of Lisa, the crazed bordello hat-check girl), but on the subject of makeup, beauty, skin care, and cosmetics . . .

True, it wasn't a certified undergraduate course like Advanced Math and Medieval History. It was offered as an extension course along with subjects like "Plumbing of All Nations;" "Life, Death and Patio Furniture;" "Stress, Personal Conflict and Auto Repair;" and "How to Talk to the Maid."

Each week the Beauty and Skin Care instructor invited a guest lecturer to speak. This week it was my turn. I was delighted. Not only would it give me a chance to mingle with younger people (See Chapter 11: "Dating Younger Men"), but I could impart years of skin care, hair care, and cosmetic knowledge. You've heard the expression, "We learn from our mistakes" . . . boy, would they learn a lot from me!

The sign outside read: "Phyllis Diller Lectures on Beauty and Cosmetics," which was like a George C. Scott course on accepting awards. Inside, the lecture hall was overflowing with coeds, and a few middle-aged students who believed I had achieved beauty and perfection, and who wanted to know how I did it. (These were not honor students.)

My opening remarks were brief and to the point.

"Hello . . . It's good to be back. The last time I was on the UCLA campus I was hired by Phi Epsilon Pi during hazing week. Incoming pledges, as part of their hazing ceremony, had to watch me streak. All except two quit school the next day. Those two committed suicide. I went to college many years ago. To give you an idea how long ago it was, we tried telephone booth stuffing, but we couldn't. The phone hadn't been invented yet!

"Okay, that says I'm old. And you people are young. You are in your prime, your sexual peak, your wonder years. You have your life and your bosoms still standing directly ahead of you. You are not yet at the age when gravity has become the enemy. You are still at that innocent age . . . you are more concerned with mid-terms than mid-life crisis; with

IT WILL JUST WRINKLE
YOUR BIRTHDAY SUIT A LITTLE

SKIN MAINTENANCE
—
PREVENTING WRINKLES

the fall of the Roman Empire than with the fall of your face. Your biggest crisis is getting your hands on a Dr. Pepper. I'm trying to get ahold of Dr. Hinkle from Cedars-Sinai.

"Cosmetically, you are the age to be envied and worshipped. Every older woman wants youthful skin. Sometimes we get it. A sixty-two-year-old friend of mine went to bed at night and prayed, 'Please God, give me skin like a teenager's.' Next day she woke up with pimples.

"I am here today to talk about cosmetics, skin care, and beauty problems. I am here as a warning . . . This is what you could become if you don't take care of yourself and start *now!* We'll now open it up to questions and answers."

Q: When did you first realize you were in trouble, cosmetically?

A: I knew I had to do something about my face when I saw a sign at the entrance to a scenic national park: "Do not litter, throw beer cans, or bring Phyllis Diller into this area."

Q: Are there any specific signs that your body is aging?

A: Yes. When you still "jiggle" . . . but the jiggling's under your *eyes.*

Q: Are you saying that after age thirty we have to fear every birthday?

A: Another birthday won't cramp your style . . . it will just wrinkle your birthday suit a little. Wrinkles are the biggest problem facing aging women today. I don't care how much surgery you have, those pesky buggers are bound to show up—sometimes in the strangest parts of your body.

Q: What exactly causes wrinkles?

A: Worry and stress! That's why my face has been perennially selected as poster girl for the Ohio State Fair Whipped Prune Festival. I worry about *everything*. I worry that:

Gary Coleman will have an affair with Susan Anton.

The White House will go Condo.

Needlepoint will replace sex.

Florence Henderson will be revealed as a Mafia chieftain.

I will be seriously injured by static cling.

Full frontal nudity will make its debut on TV soon, and the host of the first show will be Abe Vigoda.

Q: But those are silly, frivolous worries.

A: True, but there are also so many *real* problems in today's society: crime, inflation, coping, relationships, husband straying . . . that it's almost impossible for a woman's face not to look like a relief map of the Himalaya Mountains. If you don't believe me, look at this.

I then distributed a poster to illustrate the problems contemporary women go through.

MODERN WOMAN'S WRINKLES
(What Causes Them)

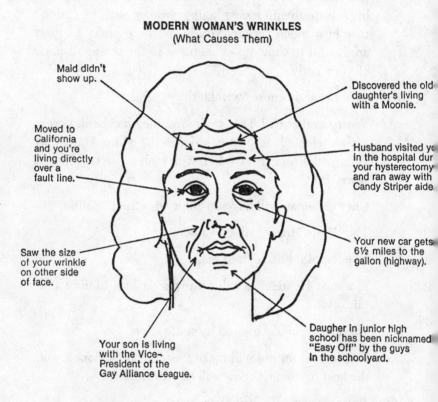

MOISTURIZER—YES! . . . AVOCADO ON YOUR FACE—NO!

The class was now getting restless and concerned. Wrinkles were starting to crease their twenty-year-old brows. One girl waved her hand anxiously.

Q: What can we do to prevent wrinkles?

A: Okay. Modern stress is causing wrinkles to gather on our faces like sailors at a Bob Hope concert. What do we do about it? Everyone has a different method. Some people exercise, some pound a pillow, some recite a mantra. Personally, I find the best way to relieve anxieties is to shout an old-fashioned curse on your enemies. Confront the object of your pent-up hostility . . . your boss, your in-law, your straying spouse, your nosy neighbor (who borrowed your coffee percolator and your husband and didn't return *either* of them) . . . simply rear back and shout at them à la Karnak the Magnificent . . .

May Too Tall Jones fall on you!

May you get an obscene phone call from your psychiatrist!

May your water bed leak!

May you get paid in nothing but Susan B. Anthony dollars!

May you invest heavily in a solar heating system and may every day be cloudy.

May your no-nonsense bra giggle!

May your son work in Hawaii as a Volcano Sweep.

May a Saint Bernard mate with your leg.

If any of the above curses don't work, you may be forced to use moisturizers and cosmetics.

Q: Do moisturizers and cosmetics really help?

A: Cosmetics can do wonders for a woman. Look what it did for Elizabeth Arden, Merle Norman, and Estée Lauder. It's made them millionaires.

Q: Is it just media hype or is it *really* possible to have a cover-girl complexion?

A: It all depends on your complexion. For three successive issues I was cover girl for *Fish & Wildlife*.

Q: Do you believe in moisturizers?

A: You've got to be kidding. They are my personal God. (Every night I kneel down with a sponge applicator and pray to Our Lady of Helena Rubenstein.)

Q: Do you take milk baths?

A: I tried it but I kept getting stuck in the bottle.

Q: I'm on a limited budget. Aren't moisturizers expensive?

A: Be creative. Improvise. During my struggling years I couldn't afford a moisturizer. I used to put yeast on my face then run through a car wash.

Q: I heard a facial of avocado, cucumber, and honey can help keep you young.

A: There are also hazards. My sister-in-law left that kind of concoction on one night. The next morning migrant

workers marched into her bedroom and were picketing her head! As a general rule I don't think it's a good idea for a woman to make her face into a salad bar.

Q: A few years back they actually came out with the news that Preparation H applied to your face tightens the skin and gets rid of wrinkles.

A: I do not highly recommend this. We women have enough beauty problems . . . We don't need help to look like an ass.

THEY ARE NOT PUNK ROCK GROUPS— THEY'RE EVEN MORE EMBARRASSING

Since this was a school I decided to slip in a little quiz. I told them to answer the following:

Varicose Veins; Stretch Marks; Sun Spots; Gray Hair; Crows Feet.

These are:
  A) Punk Rock Groups.
  B) Indian tribes who went on the warpath outside La Costa.
  C) Cosmetic problems that embarrass older women.

Unfortunately, number three is the answer. As women get older, unsightly blemishes (as opposed to the much preferred *slightly* blemishes) appear on our bodies. It is not a thrilling sight.

Q: What exactly are varicose veins?

A: I call it the Rand McNally disease. It's when your legs start looking like a road map of Eastern Europe. The thing is *never* to admit you have them. When people ask what those strange blue lines are, I tell them, "I smoked too much grass last night and had myself tie-dyed."

Q: What about facial hair?

A: I'm generally against it, except in poorer South American nations. For women with real heavy facial hair problems, I suggest industrial-strength Nair.

Q: What is cellulite?

A: That's a treatment for things that go bump in the night.

Q: Through cosmetics and surgery can *any* part of the body be made to look younger?

A: Everything except the hands. No matter how much lotion, rejuvenation cream, or "new and improved" dish-washing soap we use, hands are a sure tell-tale sign of age. There's no hiding it. Your face may say "Twenty-year-old surfer from Malibu," but your hands will say, "Little Old Lady From Pasadena."

Anytime you see a lady making her entrance into a cocktail party wearing a sexy disco dress, a tight, creaseless face and aviator gloves, you *know* she's old. Or, when an attractive lady sashays by a motel pool in a string bikini and mittens. You just *know* those are hands that have endorsed Social Security checks.

THAT OLD GRAY HAIR—
IT AIN'T WHAT IT USED TO BE

"It's not fair!" I complained to the class. "Cary Grant has gray hair and is described as "distinguished." Johnny Carson has gray hair and is described as "aging beautifully." If a forty-five-year-old actress has gray hair, she is described as a "walking canker sore."

In our society men can get away with graying naturally, women can't. Next to global war and trying to have a meaningful relationship with a disc jockey, gray hair is the one thing that ages you most.

Q: What about the salt-and-pepper look? Isn't that kind of a popular style?

A: It's okay for guys. If a woman has the salt-and-pepper look, men tend to toss you over their shoulders to avoid bad luck.

Q: Do you recommend plucking out gray hairs, one by one?

A: Not unless your hobby is pain.

Q: Then, what's the best way to hide that gray?

A: You can have it bleached, tinted, frosted, rinsed, streaked, or, if you're on an economy kick, you can date a Sherwin Williams salesman and let him playfully run a Number 6 roller through your hair. You can, of

course, also try wigs. I've tried them, and it doesn't pay to get a cheap one. Every morning I take mine out for a walk. And I have to have it wormed twice a month.

Q: What's the best shade to choose?

A: There are many attractive and trendy colors to bleach your hair. The two that I *don't* recommend are "Hudson River Green" and "Harrisburg Glowing Pink." Personally, I have my own favorite color. Years ago I sat myself down and had to make a decision. If I have only one life to live, let me live it as . . .

A) A Korean War Bride
B) One of the Osmonds
C) A blonde

The decision to be a blonde seemed the least involved and most rewarding.

Q: Phyllis, is it true blondes have more fun?

A: Hey, all I can say is Cheryl Ladd and I are blonde. One of us is having a helluva lot of fun!

4

Rejuvenation Spas and Clinics (Or, "You're Gonna Transplant a *What* Into My *What*?")

"Wouldn't it be great," I philosophized to my friend Estelle, "to stop the aging process? Wouldn't it be incredible to turn back the sands of time?"

She reflected, "In your case turning back the sands of time would take 600 strong life guards and they'd all get hernias!"

"Thank you," I told my ex-friend Estelle.

I've given a lot of thought to the subject of rejuvenation and the search for immortality. There's got to be a simple way to stop the aging process. I can't keep flying to that is-

land in the Pacific, putting on Adidas and running back
and forth across the international date line. It's not making
me any younger, and it's giving me calluses.

Maybe we can learn a lesson from those people in remote
areas of the world where they live to be over a hundred. In
the Caucasus Mountains of the Ukraine and in Pakistan's
Valley of the Hunza, the natives, through diet, exercise, climate, mental outlook, and never having to listen to Muzak
in elevators, are able to live to ripe old ages of 140 and 150.

Amazingly, these people are also able to keep active sexually. (I understand foreplay consists of walking up a moun-
tain and then rolling down on top of each other.)

I'm sure most of us would love to have the life-style of
the people of the Caucasus, but there would be problems in
paradise.

Embarrassment: When asked your age it's one thing to
say, "I'm crowding 40," but how do you say, "I'm
crowding 130," with a straight face?

Danger: Accidents are the biggest cause of death in the
Caucasus. One 122-year-old lady set fire to herself by
blowing out the candles on her own birthday cake.

Cultural Adjustment: I'm not sure I want to live any
place where the day camp is filled with 85-year-olds.

For those of you who don't want to move to the mountains of the Ukraine, there are a number of rejuvenation
clinics and spas where they have discovered ways to slow
down the aging process.

I have tried all these rejuvenation spas and I've always been optimistic about the results. I always ask the travel agent for a regular fare going and a "youth fare" for my return trip.

Each spa and clinic has its own particular approach to rejuvenation, though they all have one thing in common . . . they're expensive. Actually, though, it's just as well. Why would a poor person want to live longer anyway?

Below is a list of some of the more renowned spas and clinics around the world.

ERNEST BAUER HEALTH INSTITUTE, Berne, Switzerland. Very popular with the jet set. Patrons pay $1,000 a day to receive injections of lamb placenta. This may sound silly at first, but Dr. Bauer points out, "Have you ever seen a lamb that looked old?"

THE ISKOWITZC CLINIC, Krovney, Rumania. Dr. Sara Iskowitzc is the pioneer of "cell therapy," a process where patients are injected with human cells, taken from recently dead people. The theory here is that the patient's body will build up immunity to death just as smallpox vaccination causes the body to build up antibodies to ward off smallpox. The clinic is equipped with the latest in operating rooms and equipment, including "hazard lights." Two rather unusual rules: No mirrors are allowed and Dr. Iskowitzc can be seen for consultation only *after* sundown. Her radical treatment (also known as "coma therapy") costs $700 a day for two weeks. All unescorted ladies will be admitted free on Tuesdays.

TRIBAL
REJUVENATORS
OF
PLATA REY

SPA DE RIO PUERTA, San Juan, Puerto Rico. Founded by Pablo Espinoza, a former barber who specialized in the layered look, the spa is located on the fabled Rio Puerta, a natural spring whose waters are said to have miraculous healing properties. Patrons pay up to $3,500 to eat leafy vegetables, tureens of flounder soup, and drink six gallons of Puerta water a day. Espinoza supplements this regimen with an exercise program which consists of fighting to get into the one bathroom in the spa.

TRIBAL REJUVENATORS OF PLATA REY, South America. High in the Andes, in a village that can be reached only by goat or Cadillac Seville, is a group of Veldt tribesmen who are said to be able to rejuvenate and heal through the use of natural herbs, plants, and the spreading of Adolph's meat tenderizer over various parts of the body while chanting, "Bella bella Wella Balsam cardoza" ("You go around only once in life—grab as much gusto as you can"). This spa is especially popular with busy women executives and Everett Manheim, the famed octogenarian traveler and inventor of the pinwheel hat. Cost of treatment is $700 a day for two weeks.

GUNTHER KRAUSE HOSPITAL AND CLINIC, Berlin, Germany. Dr. Krause is the famed surgeon who believes the way to rejuvenation is through organ transplants. It was Krause who took the body of a 90-year-old French dowager and transplanted into it the kidney of a 22-year-old Milwaukee disco dancer (incidentally, without the disco dancer's consent). It was a partial success. The dowager's face remained wrinkled and immobile but her feet never stopped moving. Dr. Krause does not really want to perform these operations . . . he is only following orders.

CUT-RATE CLINICS—NO-FRILLS FACES

Obviously these exclusive spas and clinics can be enjoyed only by the very wealthy. There are some less-expensive rejuvenation clinics that are springing up—mostly in the U.S. These "mass consumption" spas use cheaper equipment, unskilled personnel, and rather "radical" bio-medical techniques. However, if price is a factor, these are for you:

THE SHICK CENTER TO STOP AGING, Pittsburgh, Pennsylvania. Through the use of aversion therapy they claim impressive results. The therapy consists of a series of intensive three-hour sessions in which a counselor shows a patient depressing slides of elderly people on park benches with pigeons perched on their heads. The theory is that if the thought of growing old becomes abhorrent enough, the patient will simply not *allow* himself to age. Strangely enough, there is a very high suicide rate among Shick Center graduates. Cost of the therapy is $300 . . . in advance!

THE NORMAN MAIN CLINIC, Santa Monica, California. Patients take off all their clothes and walk dramatically into the Pacific Ocean. The founder, silent-film star and health food freak, Fatty "Cuddles" Cummings, believes the combination of the pounding surf, seaweed paraffin, and oil slick residue against the naked skin can "shock" the body into rejuvenation. Cost is only $175 for two visits, plus $50 bail bond for causing civic disturbance.

TWO GUYS FROM MUNCIE. Founded by William and
Orville Leshman, one a Purdue pre-med student and the
other an auto pit-stop mechanic, they combined their
medical and mechanical skills to create the philosophy
behind this very popular chain of southern Indiana Body
Rejuvenation centers. Their philosophy: "You can halt
the aging process by sitting on an air hose."

5

Health...What My Friends Are Always Drinking to Before They Fall Down

Next to gold and jewelry, health is the most important thing we have.

Actually, you can't put a price tag on health. Without it you're really in bad shape . . . and you'll look it.

Somebody, I think it was either Voltaire or Joey Bishop, said, "Your body is a temple, and you'd better take care of it or your husband will worship somewhere else."

In my case . . . services have been canceled!

My health is not bad. Thank God I feel better than I look. Some people hate going to the doctor's office. I look forward to it. It's not often a man says to me, "Take off your clothes."

If we're going to stay youthful looking and have glowing vitality, we must learn all we can about pills, health products, vitamins, medicines, drugs, check-ups, skin conditioning, and whether Valium should be taken straight or otherwise. (I mash mine in with my bananas.) If we do this, we'll go into the second half of our lives fit as a fiddle . . . Of course, some of us may have a few squeaks. We can't all be Stradivariuses.

Is all this clear? If not, it doesn't matter. All I know is, if this book is ever made into a movie, I want Al Pacino to play the part of Chapter 10.

WE'VE GOT TROUBLE MY FRIENDS . . . RIGHT HERE IN LIVER CITY

I love the story of the man who went to a new doctor and complained of aches and pains. The doctor examined him and said, "There's nothing wrong with you."

"Are you sure?" questioned the man.

The doctor looked at him wearily, "I know what I'm doing. I've been a doctor for thirty-eight years."

"That may be so," said the man, "but I've been a patient for sixty-two."

Like that man, I've also been a patient for many years. This, coupled with my four years in medical school (I worked my way through as a cadaver) gives me the credentials to dispatch some good, sound medical advice.

GENERAL HEALTH TIPS

—There are some things that are bad for you and your skin . . . sun, wind, smog, crop dusting . . . try to avoid them!

—Don't walk barefoot in the rain. Walking barefoot in the rain only works for: A) incurable romantics; B) Girls in 20th-Century Fox musicals; and C) Free-play period at state mental institutions.

ACUPUNCTURE—I don't believe in it. I tried it once . . . The doctor told me to take two needles and call him in the morning.

HEADACHES—Despite Excedrin, Bufferin, and extra-strength Tylenol, some will NOT go away. For years every morning I woke up with a nagging headache—my husband!

SMOKING AND DRINKING—Moderation is the key. A glass of wine in the evening before dinner and a single cigarette after each time you have sex. I am a lady with clear lungs! I think the last time I smoked was in the New York blackout of 1966. (It was dark, he was drunk . . . he thought I was a soft lamp post.)

IRON SUPPLEMENTS—Don't overdo it! I take Geritol day in and day out. I've got so much iron in my bloodstream that I attach my earrings with a magnet.

ALLERGIES—A change of climate usually helps. Unfortunately, when I was a kid my family moved . . . the wrong way! From dry Arizona to the cold northeast! I'm now allergic to *everything*. Last Valentine's Day a male friend brought me plastic flowers. I got artificial hay fever.

RELAXING—Pamper yourself, take long naps, you deserve it. Change your schedule. Get up every morning at the crack of 11:30. You'll look better and live longer. Remember— too much work ages you. Harriet Beecher Stowe worked hard all her life . . . 18–20 hours a day burning the midnight oil. She does *not* look good today.

PILLS—My medicine cabinet is so crowded, I take the first thing that falls out. I'm now taking 13 pills a day . . . 10

of them to cure what the other 3 did to me. It's confusing —we're now in the age of wonder drugs, and we're "wondering" what some of them are doing to us! Recently I was tense and went to this young doctor who was "into" wonder drugs. He gave me a new pill. I said, "Will this relax me?" He said, "No, you'll just dig being tense."

HOME REMEDIES—"Feed a cold and starve a fever"; "Get plenty of hot water and blankets"; "Wrap a dirty woolen sock around his neck"; "If she has morning sickness, give her Tabasco sauce and slap her with an ear of corn." These are not lines from a Randolph Scott Film Festival, but are actual home remedies and cures for illness. Some make sense, others are pure superstition. My Aunt Becky used to warn me, "Phyllis, if you sleep outside in the back yard, be sure to close the gate or you'll catch a draft." Soon after this my Aunt Becky was placed in a home. Another bit of advice was, "You will avoid respiratory illness if you face the east and sneeze into a shoe." This was from my Uncle Florsheim.

After years of suffering through home remedies (the camphor balls around my chest were not thrilling for me, nor for my dates), I've learned not to believe in silly old-world cures. I live by three sound, scientifically proven health principles:

1) Beer is a brain food
2) Sitting is a great cardiovascular exercise
3) Never kiss a man who wears a hair transplant on his chest.

VITAMINS—WHERE ARE ALL
THE NEW ONES COMING FROM?

In recent years there's been more talk about vitamins than there has about One-hour-Martinizing. (In my crowd One-hour-Martinizing is a big topic. If I do well with this book, I hope to get myself a new crowd.)

We're all familiar with the basic vitamins and their values:

Vitamin A—Promotes good eyesight. Helps keep skin resistant to infection.

Vitamin B_1—Essential to the nervous system, heart, liver.

Vitamin B_2—An aid to healthy eyes.

Vitamin B_6—Important in the regulation of the central nervous system.

Vitamin B_{12}—Necessary to the formation of red blood cells.

Vitamin C—Helps heal wounds and mend fractures. Aids in resisting some types of virus and infections. Excellent in battling colds.

Vitamin D—Important in bone development.

Vitamin E—Helps protect red blood cells; may aid the circulatory system and counteract the aging process.

Vitamin K—Helps blood to clot.

Okay, these vitamins are good but when you get to a certain point in life (called panic) these vitamins are not enough! It's like putting out a forest fire with a Water Pik.

I'm waiting for scientists to come up with NEW vitamins
. . . miracle ones that would help women cope with physical ailments that are REALLY bothering them.

These are the vitamins we need:

Vitamin M—Gives you the strength to open a bottle with a
child-proof cap.

Vitamin Q_6—Won't let fat from Ding-dongs accumulate
directly on your thighs.

Vitamin J_7—For ladies in Vegas who spend twelve hours
at a time pulling slot machine levers . . .
counteracts paper cup calluses.

Vitamin P—If you sit by a stove in wintertime . . . prevents
your skin from cracking.

Vitamin Z_1—Turns your liver spots into gold Krugerrands.

MENTAL HEALTH . . . READ THIS SECTION OR I'LL KILL YOU

How we cope with things emotionally has more of an
effect on our bodies than physical problems. If a team of
physicians tells you you have arthritis, you're upset. If they
hold up the X-rays and *laugh* at your arthritis, you're more
upset.

We have to learn to relax, loosen up, and not let daily
anxieties traumatize us. As Paul Williams' agent said, "We
have to be thankful for the little things we have."

We have to be philosophical about life. Things could always be worse. It's all a matter of values. I have a needlepoint motto hanging in my breakfast nook.

WHEN WORLD WAR III IS ON THE HORIZON,
DON'T SWEAT THE KITCHEN SCUFF MARKS.

This was put up there by my housekeeper who hates to clean scuff marks.

I have since volunteered her name on the women's draft.

If we tried we could *always* find something to worry ourselves silly about. Especially me. My life is a series of regrets and ponderables. I call them "ifs."

Believe me, I would be in much better shape today:

• If I never got that kidney transplant from a bedwetter . . .

• If I were a perfect "10" (instead of a cumulative 10—five parts of me are rated "2") . . .

• If I hadn't caused that disturbance in Baskin-Robbins by asking for a thirty-second flavor . . .

• If, on my honeymoon night, my husband didn't hang out a "Please Disturb" sign on the door . . .

If, if, if, if.

We all have regrets but we can't keep wallowing in self-pity.

The healthiest thing you can do is feel GOOD about yourself. Forget the fact that you may be a total mess (some of us can't help it . . . we were born with the gene for "total messiness"). If you have to—lie!

Be like the girl singer who was on a variety show with me. She had a wig, capped teeth, false eyelashes, fake fingernails, rear padding, and a silicone job. She then went out on stage and sang, "I Gotta Be Me."

6

We All Have Certain Hungers and Desires...Squelch Them!

The beautiful, sensuous young stewardess slipped out of her blouse and slowly let her skin-tight jeans fall to the floor. It revealed a lithe and tan body, perky breasts and size 33 hips that wouldn't quit. Now, completely naked, her long blond hair cascading over her perfectly rounded buttocks, she ambled over to the bed and beckoned Larry to her. The handsome line-backer for the Chattanooga Jets smiled knowingly and slipped a firm hand onto her sleek, milk-smooth thigh. There was a strange stirring in her loins, a quivering in his groin, a twinkle in her eye, a lump in his throat and a wetness in the water bed. Larry popped open a bottle of Dom Perignon. "No—no time for that," she whis-

pered. "I'm thirsty for other things." He unbuckled his
suede Gucci belt. "Shall we do it the regular way?" "No,
surprise me," she said, eagerly. "I like surprises." Seeing the
beseeching look in her eyes he quickly slipped off his pants
and jockey shorts and then went to a drawer and pulled out
a knotted hankie, a Navy rope, a vibrator, suction cup shoes,
a photo of Debbie Boone, a papaya, a pair of exploding
socks, a rubber wet suit, and an old Perry Como album. To
the musical strains of "It's Impossible," he went to the closet
and opened it. Out came a miner with a pack mule. "Hey,
what's *this* all about?" she gasped.

Okay, now that I've got your attention, let's talk about
food and diets.

It's a subject that has been done to death. We needed
something to make you sit up and take notice.

I didn't even want to include this chapter in my book. My
publisher said, "Let's have lunch and talk about it."

He was on a unique diet . . . a combination Atkins, Still-
man, Pritikin, Scarsdale, Weight Watchers, and slow famine.
His lunch consisted of a slice of Melba toast, a half pound
of kelp, and to wash it all down, a glass of tea steam. I
said, "Is there a name for this besides "The Stupid Diet"?

He said, "It keeps me trim and healthy." He looked like
Don Knotts after six weeks in a Turkish prison.

Then, I wondered why am I putting *him* down? My history of nutrition hasn't been awe inspiring. I figured if you
are what you eat . . . I am sour milk and leftovers.

When I was a kid growing up, my eating habits were not
the best. I was the only kid on the block whose mother gave
her the Breakfast of Runners-up.

My cereal would snap, crackle, and *gag*. For a treat, on holidays we would have oatmeal on a shingle!

My home was lovable, but the food was laughable. It was often Board of Health time. Really terrible! It was like a scene out of *Oliver*. I remember my father reaching into a big pot and ladling out some strange gray-brown substance to each of us kids. I held out my bowl and begged, "Please sir, can I have LESS?"

Like all kids at that time, I was guided by the Nutrition Food Health Chart. Remember those? At every school there was a chart on the wall with a picture of four foods that, if you consumed them regularly, would give you strong bodies and glowing health for life. The foods: white bread, whole milk, eggs, and red meat.

The FDA has just placed those four foods on their Death Chart.

Do you realize that what was once "health" for me is now lunch time for laboratory Canadian rats? And *they're* spitting it up!

No wonder I look the way I do.

Okay, so what's my philosophy of food and diet? Simple. Get thinner but don't kill yourself! We all agree the thinner you are the younger you look. Audrey Hepburn looks younger than Shelley Winters; Ali McGraw looks younger than Aunt Jemima; Olivia Newton-John looks younger than Dom DeLuise. Sure, they all look good—but at what price?

I feel sorry for all those actresses and dancers who have to diet every moment of their lives. They don't know what they're missing.

They've never had a chocolate swirl ice cream cone or known the joy of an after school Twinkie with milk.

They've never had a pizza or, better yet, a pizza delivered. They've never eaten take-out Chinese food with the taste of cardboard still on their egg foo-yung.

They've never known the rapture of going to a children's birthday party and sneaking some candy corn or a Butterfinger or a jaw breaker.

They've never gone into the woods with the gang, lifted a mug, and sung, "Here's to good friends . . ."

I say, don't give up the good life but find new, inventive ways to stay slim, trim, and young looking.

Here are some "original" weight-loss suggestions. They may cost you an extra dollar or two but as Narcissus said to his best friend, himself, "You can't put a price on good looks."

EAT AIRLINE FOOD

I know a business executive who claims he goes on airlines for the food. That's like saying he buys *Playboy* for the articles.

I don't believe him.

Nobody likes airline food!

Yes, some of the major airlines do serve decent meals, but I'm suggesting taking obscure, out-of-the-way, airlines.

Carriers like Pre-Fab Airways, Matt & Bill's Airlines, Skippy's Shuttle Service, AAA (Almost Always Airlines), and the famous Flight of the Golden Taco—Illegal Alien Airways.

Travel these airlines and you're guaranteed to get meals with watery gravy, artificial toppings, MSG, food coloring, beef jerky in emulsified sauce, and weird Jell-O that will stand *still* during turbulence.

The plane may not stay up—and the meals will not stay down!

FREQUENTLY DINE
AT THEME RESTAURANTS

Regular visits to the theme or "gimmick" restaurants are guaranteed to put a halt to your appetite.

There are all sorts of these novelty restaurants springing up: A medieval restaurant (with a name like 1070 A.D.) where they have waiters and waitresses dressed like knights and wenches and the menus are printed on axes. Pirate restaurants where the salad bar is buried in a treasure chest. Instead of gold and silver, you're searching for croutons and garbanzo beans. Also, those exotic Middle-Eastern restaurants.

I went to one recently where the waiter brought out bad shish kabob. I didn't know whether to eat it or throw myself on the sword!

Japanese restaurants don't have bad food, but there are too many distractions to really digest anything properly. They have these samurai chefs wielding knives and putting on a show. I have a cheap friend who brings his newborn sons there just to be circumsized.

If the food doesn't turn you off at these places, the washrooms will. I don't mean going into them . . . I mean FINDING them!

The doors are never marked "Men" and "Women." They always have names that take a Berlitz student to decipher. In Mexican restaurants it's "Caballaros" and "Señoritas." In medieval restaurants, "Lords" and "Wenches." A lamb specialty place had "Rams" and "Ewes." My sister-in-law was stranded for three hours in a fish restaurant trying to figure out whether to go into "Fluke" or "Flounder."

HAVE FRIENDS "ROAST" YOU

Nobody has ever gained weight at a celebrity Friars' roast. It's the best diet I know. It's hard to put on pounds when you're putting on each other.

After all, how can you hold down your veal cutlet if Berle hits you with, "Phyllis Diller is now dating an Insurance Adjustor. He took one look at her and told her her body had been totalled!"

Or Don Rickles stands up and says, "We want to congratulate Phyllis Diller on her award. She has just been named, 'Miss Festering Sore.'"

I gagged on my chicken croquettes on that one!

Okay, it's hard to get a Berle, Hackett, or Rickles to roast Elvira Finsterwald of Pottstown, Pennsylvania, or Miriam Blesch of Hickory, North Carolina (actually there's a North Carolina ordinance that prevents the locust and Don Rickles from ever entering the state), but you *can* invite some friends and relatives over (particularly the ones who don't care for you), set up a dais, buy a book of stock one-liner insults and stage your own appetite depressing "roast."

For example, suppose we were roasting Doreen Lutz, a housewife of Brattleboro, Vermont. Uncle Waldo gets up and speaks first.

"They asked me to say a couple of words about Doreen . . . how about fat and boring?"

Next it's her husband's turn.

"Marrying Doreen was the second biggest thrill of my life. My *first* biggest thrill was being drafted. Hey, only kidding! I love her dearly . . . but she's fat!"

(Everybody, led by Cousin Maurice) "*How* fat is she?"

"I bought her earrings. It took three days to pierce her ears. She has more chins than the Chinese telephone directory."

Her neighbor Carlotta gets up and chimes in, "Doreen is also dull."

(Everybody) "How dull is she?"

"She delivered a eulogy . . . the corpse yawned! She spoke in Idaho near a sack of potatoes . . . their eyes started closing!"

Try and keep your food down after that.

IF YOU HAVE A STRONG
DEATH WISH—DINE HERE

The trick is to lose weight . . . not your life. It hardly takes a Jeane Dixon to predict that if you eat at certain restaurants you're going to get hurt.

Do not eat at:

· Any restaurant that features: "Cream of Yesterday" soup.

· Any restaurant that specializes in wolf pudding!

· Any place called "The Di-Gel Diner."

· Any place where it takes four minutes to eat lunch and thirty seconds to lose it!

· Any place that warms up their omelettes by "sitting on them."

· Any Chinese restaurant called "House of Wind."

· Any restaurant that features the wines of Kansas.

• Any place that rolls out a dessert cart with hazard lights.

• Any drive-in fast-food chain where, instead of a talking clown, you give your order to a giant sperm whale!

YOUNG FOOD VS. OLD FOOD

As you're cranking your shopping cart (with only two working wheels instead of three) down the supermarket aisle, or you're sitting in a fine restaurant studying the menu, be aware, not only of price, calories, nutritional value, and taste, but . . . is it old food or young food.

Nothing looks or sounds worse than going to the checkout counter and the checker yelling out, "How much for the dietetic Melba toast and the stewed prunes?" Or the waiter saying politely while stifling a giggle, "I'm sorry, Madam, we don't serve tapioca."

Remember, the image you present is more important than the food you digest.

Certain foods are young foods, certain ones are old foods. Select only young foods.

Here is a convenient guide:

A guacamole burger is young

A poached egg on whole wheat is old

Stewed prunes are old

A Lorna Doone cookie is old

A marijuana cookie is young

Saccharine is old

A Pop Tart is young

Oatmeal used to be young, now it's old

Baked flounder is old

Sanka is definitely old

Boiled chicken is very old

Skim milk is old

Mother's milk is young

Dietetic ice cream is old

A strawberry margarita is young

Dr. Brown's celery tonic is old

By the way, I know what you're thinking and it's not going to work. You *can't* mix young food and old food. Don't order poached egg with a strawberry margarita or boiled chicken garnished with a marijuana cookie.

You'll only reveal yourself to be more senile than you already are.

7

Mid-book Crisis

Henny Youngman got on stage and was rattling off his psychiatrist's jokes. "A man walked into a psychiatrist's office. He said, 'Doctor, no one pays any attention to me.' The psychiatrist said, 'Next!'" He followed this with, "Phyllis Diller walked into a psychiatrist's office. The psychiatrist took one look at her and said, 'Get UNDER the couch!'"

I heard that joke and marched off to a psychiatrist to talk about it. I walked into his office—he took one look at me and said, "Get under the couch."

Okay, that was years ago . . . Since then it hasn't bothered me. I've even become wealthy and successful looking like a nightmare. I haven't gone back to a psychiatrist because there hasn't been a need. Until *now*. You see, right now I'm going through a trauma that most authors go through at about this time in their novel.

Yes . . . I'm going through Mid-book Crisis!

It's that emotional period in an author's life when you start to wonder and question. Your book is middle-aged now . . . you're past the brilliant teenage pages . . . no longer are you in your peak twenties and thirties. You start to wonder about your potency . . . your ability to perform. Can you still satisfy the way you once did? Do the cooking jokes still have the same zing they had when you were younger? Can the one-liners about clothes, beauty parlors, shopping, and no-frills sex (the kind you have *after* marriage) still flow?

You have your doubts.

Then comes the big shock. Signs of physical age start to creep in. Little things: You notice your typewriter ribbon is starting to turn gray. Your once brand new pages are starting to get wrinkled. Your pair of once firm Thesauruses are starting to sag.

You're desperate for acceptance. You'll do *anything*. Even cheating. You start to sneak out at night and see other publishers.

Okay, I'm getting over it. I'm starting to come out of it now. I guess Mid-book Crisis is just a stage . . . something all authors go through . . . Twain, Mailer, Bombeck, and the guy who wrote "The Complete Book of Auto Repairs"— who might have been stuck after the chapter on Ball Joints and before Lug Nut Replacement.

The best thing for me now is just to forget it and work out my problems through physical fitness.

See the next chapter.

8

Exercise and Sports

DRASTIC MEASURES
FOR DRASTIC MEASUREMENTS

Exercise is not my best thing. First of all, I am not built for it. My reflexes are slower than a turtle on Sominex.

When I was bringing up my kids I was strictly a "morning exerciser." That is, until I had my first cup of coffee, I ran into walls.

Later, when my show business career got rolling, I found new ways to keep active. My two biggest exercises were moving over one seat on the "Tonight Show" (to make room for the next guest . . . once the King Family came on and I had to move over fourteen seats), and climbing to the top row of "Hollywood Squares."

My doctors told me this was not enough activity. I was about as active as a eunuch at a Playboy mansion jacuzzi party.

So, I got involved in other sports shows. I went on "Jackpot Bowling." I'll never forget my first strike. It was three alleys over. I tried for "Celebrity Tennis" . . . that's a pretty face with a lousy backhand. I wasn't good enough for *either* category.

Finally, I was invited on one of those star-studded TV extravaganzas, BATTLE OF THE OTHERWISE OUT OF WORK CELEBRITIES. Some of the events made no sense at all. I was pitted against Red Skelton and David Brenner in the "giggle-off" competition, against The Incredible Hulk in arm wrestling, and the last event was the tug-of-war.

The teams didn't seem fair. It was Suzanne Somers, Lauren Hutton, and Goldie Hawn on one side, against Ernest Borgnine, Mean Joe Greene, and myself. We won the event, but they won the camera shots and the audience cheers. I found out later that the event was called "Beauties vs. Beasts."

VIP EXERCISERS

I really couldn't take these TV sports spectaculars seriously. (I found out later that a lot of the stars *paid* someone to perspire for them.) The important thing is it was *activity*. As much as we hate it, exercise and sports *do* make you look younger, leaner and healthier.

They needn't be boring either. Everyone has their own way of getting exercise in.

Zsa Zsa Gabor has logged millions of miles just walking up and down wedding aisles.

Mickey Rooney's favorite exercise is climbing tall people.

Don Rickles works up a sweat at shopping centers . . . moving the "handicapped only" parking signs as far away from the door as possible.

Little Gary Coleman keeps fit every morning by jogging around Orson Welles.

Raquel Welch is in great shape because of me. She spends forty-five minutes a day just opening the hate mail I send her.

SELECTING THE RIGHT SPORT— OR, "MASOCHISTS, CHOOSE YOUR WEAPONS"

What's the best activity for you? I don't know. I'm really not an expert on sports. Until last year I thought "Semi-tough" was a description of my rump roasts.

I was also kind of turned off sports on my honeymoon night. My husband, who was a big sports fan, held up Olympic cards grading my performance. He flashed cards with the numbers: "3.6"; "3.2"; and "2.8," and that was just for foreplay. He didn't actually rate my sexual performance, but he did call the front desk and ask them to send up a gong.

I have learned that, no matter what sport or exercise program you choose, it should be suited to you personally. My doctor, for example, took one look at me and told me my sport should be "chasing cars."

Here are some popular sports along with my thoughts on each.

SWIMMING: Swimming is preferable to many other physical activities, especially drowning! If you can afford a swimming pool, it may be worth it for you. We bought a second-hand swimming pool, but it looks like new. The ad said it had only been swum in twice . . . by a nice clean old lady. And she never swam fast.

Just about everybody's into swimming today. There's even a swimming pool at the White House, and twice a day President Reagan takes a brisk walk across it.

JOGGING: Jogging is when you run and run and run and don't seem to go anyplace. They got the idea from Harold Stassen.

Just as "riding to hounds" is known as the sport of kings, jogging has rightly become known as the sport of morons. The good thing about jogging though is that, after doing it, at least you look like a *young* moron.

WALKING: Walking gives you tone, vigor, helps your heart, and is mainly for people who don't look fantastic in those satin jogging shorts. Let's face it . . . walking is poor man's jogging! When you look like Cheryl Tiegs, you jog. When you look like me, you walk.

Walking *must* be my sport. I've gone up to countless athletic looking young men and told them I was interested in sports. They all told me the same thing . . . "Take a hike."

SKIING: Skiing is like sex after fifty-five. It looks exciting, but it's really a struggle. I start out trying to look like Suzy Chapstick—and I end up looking like Mr. Goodwrench. They usually have to pry me off a hill. I didn't realize how dangerous the sport was until I saw the names of the slopes: "Beginners," "Intermediate," and "The Widow Maker." I figure this sport is not for anybody who still has her mittens pinned to her parka!

Besides the danger, skiing can be very expensive. Three hundred dollars for skis can be intimidating to ladies on a tight budget. Here's a money-saving hint: Let your toenails grow long and ski barefoot.

TENNIS: This sport is fun. The first time I walked on a court in tennis clothes, the teaching pro said my body had to be restrung. I pursued anyway. The pro was a good-looking guy. A cross between Robert Redford and Bjorn Borg. He was a little wary of me when I complained, "These balls are brand new and they don't bounce too well."

"You have to take them out of the can first," he explained warily. "Do you know anything at all about the rules?"

"I know all about double faults. My beauty parlor does it every week. I also know that scoring in tennis is like marrying for money . . . love means nothing!"

He quickly left me for a nubile teenager on the next court. He claimed he was going to show her his lob.

I didn't sweat it. I figured if my relationship with the pro doesn't work out, I could always start a more meaningful relationship with the ball machine.

Tennis is a great social sport. If things with the pro don't work out, you always have your husband or your boyfriend. But that could end in disaster also.

Ever notice a guy and girl playing mixed doubles?

Guy to partner:

BEFORE MARRIAGE: "You look so cute when you miss, honey."

AFTER MARRIAGE: "Hold your racquet back, stupid!"

I said it was fun. I never said it was easy.

GOLF: The easiest sport of all. You simply line up your putt, keep your arm steady, your eye on the ball and then lean in and hit it. With any luck you should make it through the windmill hole in four or five strokes. The loop-the-loop may be tougher.

As far as *regular* golf courses, forget it!

SIX SPORTS TO AVOID—
OR, "THE BONES YOU SAVE
MAY BE YOUR OWN"

Naturally, there is a risk involved in any sport or exercise. We all, at one time or another, get saddle sore, tennis elbow, jogger's knee, snorkel face, and Mah-Jong tile wounds (ivory can hurt when thrown by an irate "West"). What we should try to avoid are the more dangerous sports. Scrapes and bruises are one thing . . . it's fun when friends sign your cast . . . it's not as much fun if they sign your *casket*. Here are some sports to definitely avoid.

SWORD FIGHTING: This is a particularly risky sport for people without agility, or without a sword.

SKY DIVING: An interesting little sport. You jump out of a plane at 10,000 feet and you head for a little black dot on the ground. If you don't pull the ripcord in time, it's you!

POLE VAULTING: Not recommended unless: A) You're a prisoner; B) You're desperate to escape from your husband and it's worth it to leap over the condominium wall!

HOT-TUB SITTING: Trendy, but can be risky. I have a hot tub that seats six—drowns eight!

LION HUNTING: If you *must* go, take somebody tough with you. The only time I went on a safari, it was with Arnold Schwarzenegger. When the lions saw him they rolled up *their* windows.

DRAG RACING: Aside from the fact that it's dangerous, there isn't that much exercise involved. Besides, who would want to race while wearing clothes of the opposite sex?

CLIFF DIVING: Acapulco is famous for divers jumping from its rocky cliffs into the water four hundred feet below. If the idea of something on the rocks with a little water on the side appeals to you, I suggest you call Dean Martin and forget about Mexico.

WOULD YOU BUY A USED SKI POLE FROM THIS MAN?

As I mentioned earlier, sports-teaching pros can be quite attractive and exciting. These macho guys can really turn you on as they show you how to grip a racquet, swing a club, get out of a chair lift, or ease into a nautilus machine.

But beware! There are many charlatans out there—con guys who hang around the courts, clubs, and slopes—who are passing themselves off as pros.

Be suspicious of:

· Any skiing pro who wears a pinky ring, looks like Rodney Dangerfield, and calls himself "Heshy."

· Any tennis pro who strings his racquet with used bra straps.

· Any golf pro who likes to snort polyester and keeps falling out of the cart.

· Any health club instructor who straps himself in the machine with you and whispers, "I see you're Nautilus—I'm Aquarius."

· Any golf pro who keeps in his golf bag a 3 iron, a 4 iron, an electric vibrator, and a bucket of oysters.

· Any tennis pro who thinks a double fault is something that increases the chance of an earthquake.

TV EXERCISE SHOWS—
I'D TURN THE SET OFF,
BUT I DON'T
HAVE THE STRENGTH FOR IT!

I've watched every single TV exercise show. Personally, I'd rather be in bed reading "The History of the Blister." These exercise shows usually feature a sensational-looking girl instructor in gorgeous skin-tight leotards (you're in a ratty bathrobe and the 1958 slippers with marmalade stains) . . . and they claim they can get you in terrific shape. What they actually succeed in doing is making the less lithe among us very depressed.

The main reason TV exercise shows never appealed to me was, it was impossible to do in my house. I could never find enough clear space on my living room floor to lie down and do the exercises. In fact, half the time, in all the mess, I couldn't find the television.

The last time I watched an exercise show, the program was interrupted in the middle for a bulletin about a nuclear leak. I heard the words "leg lift," "pull up," and then "melt down." I never watched an exercise show again.

Maybe it's better if I don't do strenuous exercise anyway. After all, I'm at an age when my back goes out more than I do.

9

Tips on How to Appear Young—Without Surgically Removing, Peeling, Waxing, or Exploding Anything

What are the three most common lies told in the English language?

"I just put your check in the mail."

"Yes, darling, I'll still respect you in the morning."

"You're not getting older—you're getting better."

The guy who thought up this last one was also undoubtedly a look-out at Pearl Harbor and president of the "Man Will Never Fly Society." He was *wrong!* Let's face it. As you get older the only thing you get better at is lapsing into a coma.

We talked about plastic surgery, wrinkle creams, food, diet, vitamins, and exercise, but there are *other* less painful ways to delay the road to senility and the pathway to Seizure City . . . We can do it by changing our life-style. Yes, start gearing yourself to a young way of life . . . thinking young, talking young, dressing young, and above all, never showing proof of your real age.

LOVE IS NEVER HAVING TO SAY YOU'RE FIFTY

There are some documents in our life that, unfortunately, reveal how old we are. Birth certificates, passports, driver's licenses, citizenship papers. These papers, along with the orders to burn the Reichstag, the Bruno Hauptman ransom note, the orders for the Spanish Inquisition, and the network pink slip that canceled "Gunsmoke" rank as the most dreaded documents of all time.

The fact that the initials of the words birth certificate are B.C. is more than a coincidence . . . it's an omen!

I find showing my birth certificate about as much fun as a leaky colostomy bag.

Here are just a few of the things I'd rather do than show proof of my age:

Sell my first born.

Set my nose hairs on fire.

Be fitted for a birth control device with Crazy Glue.

Throughout my long . . . oops . . . short life, I've done

what I could to disguise proof of age. My driver's license has had more rewrites than a third-rate TV soap opera. My birth certificate has had more alterations than a Weight Watcher's designer jeans.

It is, of course, illegal to change the actual date of birth on documents, but the seasoned pro finds clever ways of detracting, disguising, and confusing the documents . . . *and* the people reading them.

"Miss Diller, what is this ink blotch covering the date of your birth on your passport?"

"My Bic exploded."

"Before we issue you this insurance policy we need to know your age."

"Let's just say I'm somewhere between Susan Anton and Susan B. Anthony."

"You'll have to be more specific."

"Okay, I'm twenty-three going on death."

"We'll need a birth certificate."

"I don't have one."

"Everyone has a birth certificate."

"I was raised by a band of Gypsies. They were lovely, colorful people, but they didn't keep records."

"Gypsies raised you?"

"They stole me from my real parents. The ones who *really* raised me."

"Who were they?"

"A pack of wolves."

"I know you're a comedienne, Miss Diller, but this whole thing is a little silly."

"Okay, here's my birth certificate."

"You were born July 17, 1947?"

"That's right."

"Are you sure? Uh . . . is that a four or a one?"

"It's a four. Trust me."

Keep in mind that no matter how much we disguise and camouflage, there are certain document "giveaways" that will not fool them. Your document is old if:

• It's written in Latin.

• They ask for proof of your age and you unfurl a parchment.

• Your driver's license has a picture of you in auto goggles.

• Your auto is insured against collision, theft, and Indian raids.

• Your insurance company is Mutual of Babylonia.

• Your license is not issued from a state but instead says, "Territory" as in "Territory of Montana."

Okay, we've seen how to alter our birth certificates and driver's licenses . . . now let's alter our life-styles.

LIFE-STYLE OR LIFE "STILL"

Your life-style is the total image you project to those around you. Is it a young, exciting life-style or an old, doddering one? Are you contemporary? Are you with it? Are you living life in the fast lane? Do you grab for all the gusto you can get? . . . Or is it impossible because your hand is covered with an oven mitt?

Which is it? Do you read *Rolling Stone* or do you sit in bed at night with a glass of warm milk and browse through *The Dead Sea Scrolls*? Is whip and chill part of your food or sex budget? Do you still say words like "snazzy" and "my goodness"? Is excitement for you dialing "O" for operator?

Do you put on your "threads" and get into your "wheels," or do you slip into your nylon stockings with a seam and crank up the Tin Lizzie? How you look, what you wear, what you say—all reveal something about you. Which explains why I'm often invited to Forest Lawn to give the lecture: "Phyllis Diller Speaks on Plasma." My life-style is about as exciting as a torn pocket.

But you can learn from my mistakes. The trick is to *always* act and think young. We've seen that certain foods say "young" and certain foods say "old." The same thing applies to these other areas.

CARS

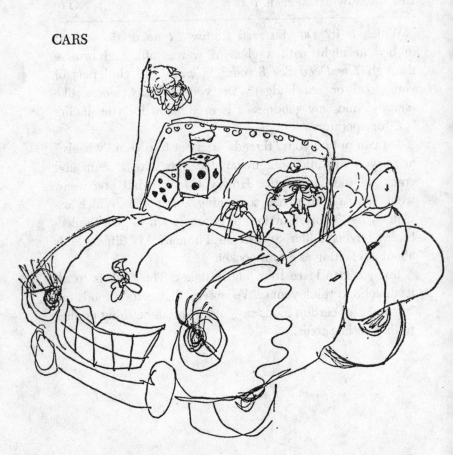

Nothing says image like the automobile we drive. If you're driving along in an open convertible with your hair blowing in the wind, that says young. If you stop the car and run out to pick up your hair, that says old.

YOUNG: Porsche, Trans Am, MG, Souped up '72 Chevy with wire wheels.

OLD: Nash, Studebaker, Hupmobile, WW II Tank, Hearse, any car whose horn goes "ooga-ooga."

CAREERS:

YOUNG AND GLAMOROUS: Stewardess, model, bunny, art student, dental assistant, disco dancer.

OLD: Movie theater matron, mid-wife, Wac, Conga instructor, file clerk in a bicycle-built-for-two repair shop, spinner of flax into gold (old, but can make you rich—the gig may be worth it).

NAMES:

YOUNG: Debbie, Carri, Teri, Tracy, Skye, Lori, Chastity, Destiny.

OLD: Agnes, Agatha, Bess, Martha, Miriam, Mamie, Gertrude, Helen . . . Any name that sounds like an ex-President's wife.

NOTE: Since the trend today is to end all those cute young names with an "I" like Debbi and Teri, if you're burdened with one of those mature "nineteenth century" names, simply change the spelling and add an "I" at the end.

Agnes becomes Agni; Martha—Marthi; Agatha—Agathi

VOCABULARY:

If you still think "dropping acid" is an accident in a chemistry lab, "sharing a pad" is borrowing someone's notebook paper, and "uppers" are a train compartment, you're in trouble on this one.

There are certain phrases that are in and others that are out. We have to be constantly wary of letting telltale expressions slip out that may reveal we are at an age when furniture dealers will soon start bidding on our legs.

AVOID SAYING:

AT A TRAVEL DISCUSSION: "I loved London, adored Paris, but I'll tell you this . . . there's nothing like being back in the good old 48."

AT A BASKETBALL GAME: "Don't they use the peach basket anymore?"

IN A DEPARTMENT STORE: "Excuse me, in what section would I find 'old oaken buckets'?"

AT A GROUP-ENCOUNTER SESSION: "I still have deep-rooted traumas. Maybe it's because, as a kid, I was dragged under by a steamboat!"

AT A POLITICAL DISCUSSION: "Don't worry. The League of Nations will get us out of this."

These faux pas and also these slips of the tongue are to be avoided like the plague . . . which *also* is to be avoided! Don't ever mention you have any diseases that say "old." "I'm sorry, I won't be in today. I've got Potato Famine" is *not* the excuse to call into the office. Also tacky are any mention of consumption, bubonic plague, and Panama Canal fever. If you *must* get sick, try to get one of the hip "young" diseases . . . herpes, mononucleosis, or Saturday Night Fever.

You'll feel much better about it.

DRESSED TO MAIM

"Of all the things a person wears, clothes are the most important."

—RIP TAYLOR TO PHYLLIS DILLER
NOVEMBER 5, 1972

The great designer Oscar de la Renta once asked me, "Phyllis, do you dress to please others or to please yourself?"

At least I think that's what he asked me. He was speaking Italian at the time. He may very well have been saying, "Is that really your outfit or was there an explosion at a pizza factory?"

Anyway, in answer to that unspoken question, it's obvious I dress to please myself. Others are not pleased.

Let's face it, I am to clothing what George Burns is to singing. I am the Mount St. Helens of fashion . . . I'm a disaster!

I was once thrown out of a party because I wasn't dressed properly. It was in Spike Jones's home.

Why do I dress this way? I am making my own personal fashion statement. I am saying to the world, "Every day can be Halloween."

Even sexy clothes don't work. I once wore a low-cut gown, walked into a party, and the onion dip turned bad. It's frustrating that revealing clothes won't work for me because today on our "let it all hang out" society, anything goes. At a singles club recently a young lady walked in in a daring two-piece outfit . . . shoes.

Some of us have to face up to the fact that we are not fashion models. Nobody has ever asked me to turn around

and "show them my Underalls." Nobody has ever invited me
to pose seductively in a Calvin Klein jeans ad. Can you
imagine me lying there, fanny up, like Brooke Shields? "Hi,
this is Phyllis Diller. If my jeans could talk they'd plead for
mercy."

My outfits seem to inspire passionate feelings in everyone.
Bob Mackie, the brilliant and usually gentle fashion designer, recently approached me in the hallway of CBS.
"Phyllis," he told me, "I've never seen you dressing better
. . . and it's a shame." He then proceeded to strangle me
with bugle beads.

I may dress badly. But the important thing is, now I dress
young.

GAYS AREN'T THE ONLY THING
THAT SHOULD BE COMING OUT
OF THE CLOSET

Putting together a "young" wardrobe is no easy feat. Start
by going through your closets and throwing out every piece
of clothing that even remotely smacks of "old." I'm talking
about such items as:

Veiled hats

Orthopedic shoes

Veiled orthopedic shoes

Shawls

Bustles

Anything made of buffalo

I also find it a wise policy to discard any item of clothing
which bears the insignia of the Confederacy. Any items

you're not sure about, better to throw them out. Or you can give them to the Salvation Army or UNICEF, though personally I think that's cruel. Those people have enough problems—why make them dress in poor taste, too. Would you want it on your conscience that somebody dressed in your clothes is the laughing stock of Bangladesh?

If you're going to dress young, you must shop at young stores. After all, you're not going to find cut-off jeans and tube tops at a place called Senile la Mode. Also when shopping large department stores it's psychologically helpful to seek out young "sounding" clothing sections: "Junior World," "The Campus Shop," "Teen Togs." Avoid departments with names like "Ambulatory Fashions," and "One Step Before The Grave Boutique." Above all, avoid any shopping center called the "Menopause Mall."

T-SHIRT MANIA

You may not have ever thought of making a $4.98 T-shirt part of your fashion ensemble, but you should. Personalized T-shirts are the hottest thing since pitted olives.

You can look young, trendy, fashionable, and make a statement on your chest. Things like, "Have a Nice Day," "I'd Rather Be Sailing," "Save Water—Shower with a Friend."

I love them. I browsed in the T-shirt store with my fiancé every day for two weeks. We had a lot of fun picking out ecological slogans and personalized messages. In fact, I made up a bunch of my own. I decided to have a different statement for different occasions.

To a TV studio I wore, "Free Chuck Barris." To a woman's group I wore, "Support E.R.A.—Hire a Broad." To a psychology convention I had printed on my T-shirt, "What Is the Meaning of Life?" (Answer on My Panty Hose).

The best one I saved for last. It said simply, "If It Feels Good, Do It."

That night my kid put scrambled eggs in my bedroom slippers, my son punched his math teacher, and my fiancé ran off with the girl from the T-shirt store.

TO BRA OR NOT TO BRA— THAT IS THE QUESTION

Certain people should never wear clothes without a bra. Dolly Parton is two of them. I'm another. I once went braless and wore a peek-a-boo blouse. It was embarrassing. First they'd peek . . . then they'd boo!

No question about it. The no-bra look is definitely *the* young, swinging look. But it's not for everyone.

You must be careful that what's swinging is the look and not *you*. The best way to decide whether you can handle the no-bra look is to try the pencil test.

Just place a pencil under your breast and see if it drops to the floor (the pencil, not your breast). If the pencil falls to the ground, you don't need a bra, you're home free, and I hate your guts.

You do need a bra, however, if:

A)   The pencil is crushed beyond recognition.

B)   You have to use a yule-log for your test.

My test was a total disaster. I'm still trying to retrieve last winter's firewood from under my left boob.

MAKING DO (SORT OF) WITH WHAT YOU HAVE

If you're just too self-conscious to wear young clothes, or you can't afford a whole new wardrobe, there are some things you can do with your present wardrobe to make yourself appear younger. For example:

· Air brush disco colors on your orthopedic shoes

· Disguise your hearing aid so that it looks like a transistor radio

· Put glitter dust on your cane

· Jazz up your wheelchair by adding racing stripes on the side

· Have braces put on your false teeth

· Finally, wear a T-shirt that flaunts a message from your own generation. Things like, "Avoid Excitement—Marry a 72-Year-Old Widow," and "I Went Through the Changes, Did You?"

10

Can Sex Keep You Young?
(And Other Silly Questions)

It's hard to believe that in these days of X-rated motels, jiggle television, and sexual relief through vending machines . . . that some women can be sexually deprived, but it's *true*.

A few years ago when the sexual revolution started I was on the casualty list. I was on the losing side. A lot of my parts went AWOL.

Absolutely nothing was happening in my marriage. I nicknamed my water bed, *Lake Placid!* "Our song" was "Taps."

I guess it's the times. A lot of middle-aged men are on a health kick these days. They don't drink, they don't smoke, and according to a lot of wives that's not *all* they don't do.

FOREPLAY IS NOT A GOLF COURSE

There have been a lot of changes in sexual attitudes and codes the last few years. (For instance, did you know it is illegal in the state of Kansas to have heavy petting during a dust storm?) For those of you (like me) who may have forgotten what's what, take this quiz and see how much you can remember.

The answers should be obvious. By the way, these questions are excerpted from my upcoming book, *The Joy of Remembering*.

- 1. A man's sexual powers diminish rapidly after . . .
    - A)   Age 70
    - B)   Johnny Carson's monologue
    - C)   You short sheet his bed

- 2. You can get pregnant if . . .
    - A)   A male's sperm fertilizes your egg
    - B)   A prince kisses you on the brow and awakens you
    - C)   You dance too close to a man who wears a leisure suit and smokes Cuban cigars

- 3. Vitality and lust are . . .
    - A)   Two prerequisites to sex
    - B)   A team of accountants on Fire Island
    - C)   The names of Cher's two youngest children

- 4. Foreplay is . . .
    - A)   A new pong game

B)   A golf course

C)   A new TV series starring Ted Bessel

- 5. A well-known aphrodisiac is . . .
    - A)   A bucket of oysters
    - B)   High school cafeteria lunch meat
    - C)   Parmesan cheese in the shape of Bo Derek

- 6. Sex is incredible with a male partner when . . .
    - A)   He's warm
    - B)   He's affectionate
    - C)   He has the hiccoughs

- 7. After an orgy it's impolite to ask . . .
    - A)   Do you validate?
    - B)   Do you live around here?
    - C)   Where can I wash up?

ANYTHING GOES

Jimmy Carter found lust in his heart. Others can find it in the Philadelphia Yellow Pages. The point is, now, here in the enlightened 1980s we ought to be able to FIND IT—SOMEPLACE!

Yes, this is the era of "anything goes." You can try things that were unheard of back in the Victorian era—or even the 1950s.

We can add excitement by experimenting with new ways

. . . new techniques . . . instead of dim lights, make love to a lava lamp; instead of perfume, spray a little "nerve gas" behind each ear; instead of dating one guy, invite a SWAT Team up to your apartment.

Sexual fantasies can also be a great release. Some people are turned on by sexual fantasy. I know *I* am. I'm a firm believer in Kraft-Ebing. In fact, one of my fantasies is spreading their Cheese Whiz all over my body. My two other favorite fantasies are:

- 1) I am a jock strap hanging from Burt Reynolds' shower stall.

- 2) Myself, Robert Redford, and Evelyn Wood, the speed-reading lady, are in bed together. We have the motel room for an hour. Redford quickly runs his fingers horizontally across her body and finishes in two minutes. The rest of the time he spends with me.

IMPOTENCY—CAN THEY CURE IT? DO YOU REALLY WANT THEM TO?

These days men in the bedroom are like Bob Hope at the peak of his Army base visits . . . they're expected to perform constantly. (I was going to say, "They're expected to be 'on' all the time, but it will never get out of these parentheses.) Some men *can't* perform constantly—especially if they're older, they're under stress, and/or they've gotten some bad news . . . like they've just been notified their house has been selected as a Neutron Bomb test site.

If your man is under stress, be patient with him. Learn

what to say and what not to say. Certain things are definite turn-offs. You'll only make him more impotent if you say:

- Are you quite finished?

- Would you believe right now I'm cleaning my oven?

- Gosh, with something that size I ought to take you to Small Claims Court.

- Thank you, that'll be one hundred dollars, please.

Also, certain words are turn-offs. These are *not* words to whisper in his ear at the precise moment of climax.*

- molasses

- sitz bath

- bear down

- feeble

Above all, no matter how bored you are, if he asks, "How was it for you?" Don't reply, "How was WHAT for me?"

SEX AFTER A HEART ATTACK? (OR: QUICK . . . DO I CALL MASTERS & JOHNSON OR JOHNSON & JOHNSON?)

What about sex with older men? Are you kidding? As a charter member of the Any Port in a Storm Society, I say grab it.

---

* If you're lucky enough to have one. If you are, you're eligible to join "The Women Who Have Climaxed Club"—Battle Creek, Michigan. Membership is now 26.

A word of caution, however. Doctors point out that sexual activity should continue until death . . . but not during it!

If your man has had a recent heart attack, we must tread carefully.

You may seem too over-anxious and inconsiderate if:

· You feed him aphrodisiacs intravenously

· You try to jump start his pacemaker

· You whisper, "This could be your last one. Let's make it good."

DILLER'S LAWS OF SEX AND ROMANCE

I have failed Philosophy more times than I have failed the Miss California Nubile Teenager's competition. The one item I *do* remember is that for centuries philosophers have been trying to teach us that some element of the universe is working in accord with some immutable rule.

Principles like Murphy's Law: "If anything can go wrong, it will."

There are others that I like . . .

The Marlin Perkins Law: "Never make a belt out of a rattlesnake until you're sure it's dead."

The Bloomingdale's Law: "At a sale, the only dress or suit that you like and that fits is not the one on sale."

I have come up with some laws and rules that I hope will help you deal with your sex and love life. God knows (unfortunately), they're too late to help mine.

- If anyone can get tired, he will.

- The bigger they are the smaller they are.

- The more beautiful the single red rose he brings you, the more gorgeous the tramp he's fooling around with.

- You can count the romance dead if he drinks champagne from your slipper and chokes on a Dr. Scholl's corn pad.

- The greater the size of his tattoo, the greater the number of visits you should make to the gynecologist.

- If you're reading *The Joy of Sex*, and he's reading *The Joy of Running*, the more likely you are to wake up with sneaker tread marks on an erogenous zone.

- If your mother takes you aside and tells you there are two sex positions for a woman—"under" and "beneath"— get a new mother.

- The greater his desire to wear a Charles Bronson mask to bed, the less equipped he will be to handle serious financial matters.

11

Dating Younger Men or Thank God Robbing the Cradle Is Not a Punishable Offense

In case you haven't heard, there's a new fad going around that's more stimulating than jogging, more daring than hang-gliding, and more sizzling than Pop Rocks. No, I'm not talking about nude accounting. The fad I'm referring to is women taking on young lovers.

It's amazing how things have changed. Middle-aged women now openly eye young men's behinds as they walk down the street, when not that long ago, the only buns they cared about were the kind you dunk in gravy.

It's no wonder the trend is catching on. If you ask me, young lovers are the best thing that's happened to women since latex. A young lover has so many advantages over a middle-aged one, it's like trying to compare the Wright Brothers' plane to Apollo XI.

As you've seen in the previous chapter, I've gotten to an age where sexual excitement is taking out a frozen dinner and reading the instructions, "Fold back foil to expose potatoes and dessert." A young lover can change all that.

Here are some basic advantages of taking on a young lover:

- When making love, young men have much better concentration and memories than older men. (Rodney Dangerfield claims he's gotten to the point in life where he loses his place during sex.)

- With a young lover, foreplay is only the *beginning*.

- A young man will not embarrass you by going to a fancy restaurant and ordering "bulk."

WHERE TO FIND HIM

Probably the best place to meet an attractive young man is either at a disco or singles bar. But I warn you, these places can be very intimidating. The first time I walked into a disco, I saw all those blinking red and blue lights, and ran into the bathroom in a panic. I thought I was having a "flash."

You can't just walk into a disco. You have to "make an entrance." You have to dazzle them with your costume. I did.

I wore my pink ankle boots, my see-through plastic pants, my no-nonsense bra, my green feather boa, and white evening gloves. (I prefer mittens, but I didn't want to risk tripping on the string.)

I walked over to the bar and ordered a Singapore sling. They made it just the way I like it—strong, and with an umbrella. I struck a match against my shoe, lit up a Camel, and stood by the bar looking cool, calm, and I thought, very Charlie's Angelish.

For some reason the young men ignored me. You'd think I had Legionnaires' Disease. One guy walked right past me and up to a young blonde in a tube top. He looked her straight in the tube and said, "What's your sign?"

"Leo," she replied.

"Yeah, I thought I was picking up Leo vibes. So what are you into?"

"Ending hunger by the year 2000 and Quaaludes," she replied.

The next thing I knew, they were walking out together.

I decided to take matters into my own hands. I was frustrated. I had to take *something* into my hands. There was a group of three absolutely gorgeous young men at the bar. I figured they heard the "Hi, what's your sign" line more times than Zsa Zsa's heard "The Wedding March," so I decided to hit them with some offbeat lines that might get their attention.

"Hi, my rash cleared up."

"Did you know that in a previous life I was Theodore Roosevelt?"

"I have a tattoo of Merv Griffin somewhere on my body. . . . Care to look for it?"

"This is the year of the child—would you like to have one?"

When all this fails, and it usually does, I end up with the direct, straight-forward approach.

"Hi, I'm Phyllis Diller. I'm a very wealthy woman. Perhaps you've seen me in films."

"Oh, yes. Weren't you in *Coma?*"

Fortunately, discos and single bars aren't the only places to meet young men. In fact, young men are literally everywhere. You just have to take the initiative.

SUPERMARKETS

Box boys are not only helpful and courteous, they also make excellent lovers. They do have one drawback, however. When making love, they have a tendency to put you on top with the other light things.

There's no quicker way to turn off a box boy than to buy items like Geritol, Polident, Ace bandages, cane wax, and industrial-strength pitted prunes. You might as well get on the intercom and announce, "Old geezer on aisle twelve." Likewise, cashing your Social Security check at the check-out stand is also a mistake.

I've found that the best approach to take with a box boy is to flatter him. Compliment him on his double bagging. Tell him how much you love a man in a smock. Thank him for being so gentle with your melons. He'll get the message.

GAS STATIONS

A young gas station attendant can solve your energy needs in more ways than one. In these days of gas slow-downs and oil shortages, *all* women are coming on to gas station employees. You'll have to stand in line not only to get gas but to get an attendant. Here are some ways to attract his attention:

- Tell him your car only gets eleven *feet* to the gallon. Can he stop it from "guzzling" so much?

- Wear a burnoose, a veil, and talk to him in Arabic. He'll think you own the station.

THE LANGUAGE OF THE YOUNG (OR: HOW TO TALK THEIR JIVE LIKE A REGULAR HEP CAT)

If you intend to have a long-term relationship with a young person, sooner or later you're going to have to talk with him, even if it's just to say, "Is that my foot, or have we just violated Tennessee law?"

The young have a language all their own. When they hit you with phrases like, "Where's it at?"; "I'm into my own thing"; "I'm getting my head together"; you should never respond with "Hubba-hubba," or "Golly, you're nerts!"

To avoid embarrassment and slashed tires on your Nash Rambler, here are some guidelines for communicating with today's young.

WHEN HE SAYS:	IT'S WRONG TO SAY:
Do you wanna rap?	Okay, but not across the face. It cost me a fortune.
How do you feel about S&M?	It's good, but I prefer Safeway.
Want to sit in my hot tub?	You have a stolen tub?
What do you think of the "Midnight Special"?	My favorite. I love prunes.
Let's turn on. I have a roach in my car.	That's okay. I have some Black Flag in my purse.
Why don't we go to my place and make granola?	We're both grown-ups. You can say "love."
Do you have any hash?	No, but there's some Spam in the pantry.
Do you mind if I hit on you?	Okay, but not across the face. It cost me a fortune.

IF YOU'VE GOT HIM, FLAUNT HIM

Once you've hooked onto an attractive young dude, don't hide him. Bring him everywhere. Display him like a trophy. Pretend he's a piece of jewelry and you're Sammy Davis, Jr. Other ladies will *die* when they see you enter that party with your surfer/lover. However, the introductions may be a little awkward.

"Doctor and Mrs. Fielding, this is my date, The Toad."

I could tell The Toad was not totally at home at the Fieldings'. He cornered me near the cheese dip, "What's this green, stringy stuff on the floor?" he asked.

"It's called carpeting," I replied.

"It can't be. It doesn't have any holes in it."

When dinner was served there were eleven glasses of wine and one Jack Cola. What's worse, it was a bad year.

CAN THEY EVER BE TOO YOUNG?

Yes, they can. After all, you don't want to be going through change-of-life the same time your date is going through change-of-voice.

There are some sure-fire ways to tell if your date is too young for you.

- Can he fly for half-fare?

- Are his love letters to you written in Crayola?

- Is his bedroom wallpapered in a clown motif?

- Do his pajamas have feet?

- When you ask him a question, does he raise his hand before answering?

THE DISADVANTAGES OF SEX WITH A YOUNGER MAN (OR: GIVE ME A SECOND, I'LL THINK OF SOMETHING)

Believe it or not, sex with a younger man is not all a bed of roses. There are some drawbacks. For example:

He may expect you to respond.

Young people are wildly experimental. They may want you to try more than one position. This would completely throw me because I'm used to the one standard position—woman above, swinging from the chandelier, wearing a wet suit.

He may have mirrors all over the bedroom, and you may actually *see* some of the disgusting things you're doing!

If he asks you to hop into his waterbed, it could be embarrassing explaining you have to take a Dramamine first.

They're quick. It's all over before Carson finishes his monologue.

You may have to explain parts of your body he may not have seen before.

HE: What's that hickey on your shoulder?
YOU: It's not a hickey. It's a vaccination.
HE: A *what?*

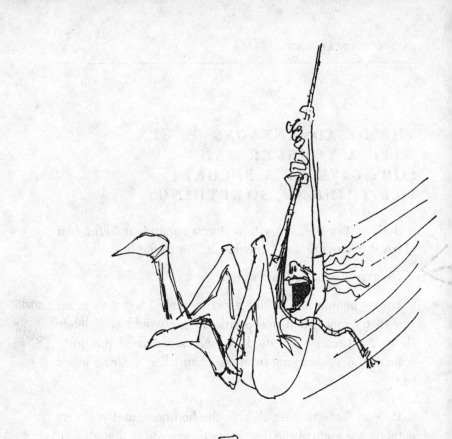

YOU: A vaccination. Something used to ward off disease.

HE: What's that one for?

YOU: Diphtheria.

(HE LOOKS AT YOU STRANGELY)

YOU: In case the Kaiser's troops attacked. We had to be protected.

12

Death...
Is It Healthy for You?

Okay, as the man working the Human Cannon Ball event said as his flying sister overshot the stadium bleachers and disappeared into another zip code, "We gave it our best shot . . . but it wasn't quite good enough."

You tried it all. You tried the spas, clinics, face-lifts, diets, exercise, and miracle vitamins. You changed your name from Agatha to Tracy, traded your Nash for a Moped, and wearing your no-bra tube top you cruised Club Med in Oahu hoping to pick up a bronzed twenty-six-year-old.

You've been about as successful as a PLO Speaker at a Bar Mitzvah.

Welcome to the "It's Not That Easy Club."

At one point some of us might have to come to terms with the fact that we're . . . yes, I'll say it . . . OLD!

How can you tell? Well, there are some telltale signs. You know you're getting older when:

Friends start talking louder to you.

· You are suddenly receiving more "get well" cards than "junk mail."

· Your favorite exercise is a good brisk sit.

· You get winded gumming a mint.

· It takes a half hour each morning to "wake up your leg."

· You have to hire someone to read this list to you.

There'll be *other* little signs of senior citizenville that won't thrill you:

· Certain words that start creeping into your conversations. Words like "spry," "plasma," "salt free," and "fast, temporary relief."

· You will be invited to attend seminars on "Death Planning," "Nutrition Education," and "Grief Therapy."

· You'll suddenly forget things. One of your new hobbies will be finding your lap.

Your life-style will change . . .

·) "Regularity" will become more important than "popularity."

· The label that says, "Designed by Halston" will have less value than the label that says, "Designed in cooperation with leading orthopedic surgeons."

· You'll realize that hot flash and the chills is not the name of a new rock group.

You may be saying, "Wait, I can't be getting old. There's so much left to do. I haven't found myself yet." I look at it this way—if you haven't found yourself by sixty-five, somebody better point!

You can handle your final years in one of two ways: You can grow old gracefully, or you can do it like me.

· I panic!

· I handle it about as well as a church entertainment committee handles wet T-shirt contests.

When ecology-minded people mention fossil fuels I start to take it personally.

At times, lately, I've been seen walking despondently down the supermarket household appliance aisle singing the excerpt from *My Way* ". . . Now the end is near, and now I face the final curtain . . ." And then throwing myself on the display of Phillips Head Screwdrivers!

Friends shake their heads sadly and say, "It's not easy for Phyllis at her age . . . She's approaching twenty-two for the third time."

HIGHLIGHTS OF GROWING OLD

I've pointed out some of the drawbacks to old age, but it's not all oatmeal, liver spots, and mobile chest-X-ray trucks. Let's take a look at some of the highlights of aging.

HIGHLIGHTS OF OLD AGE

Okay, there ARE no *highlights*. There are, however, certain advantages to old age:

- You will not be asked to join the Coast Guard.

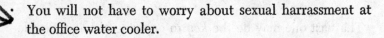

- You will not have to worry about sexual harrassment at the office water cooler.

- Boy Scouts will help you across the street.

- People will start cutting your meat for you.

- You are *allowed* to be eccentric.

OLD AGE CAN BE FUN—
FORGET THE TWO PARAMEDICS
LOITERING IN YOUR HALLWAY

That last one may be the *key* to enjoying old age. People will accept weird behavior from old people. You can do all the bizarre things you couldn't do when you were thirty-five. (If you still have the strength.) I have one aunt who sits alone in the attic and talks to herself . . . then complains of hearing voices.

You can get away with this stuff when you're ancient. People will accept it. When you're eighty-six you can ask to be "carried places" and your nieces and nephews will do it.

Go with it! Make your final years your wonder years.

MAKING OUT YOUR WILL

Last wills and testaments are usually serious, rigid documents. They needn't be. Have fun with it! It doesn't have to read like an obituary column. Make it read like *Mad* magazine. Just think of the reactions of your relatives as the lawyer reads:

· Being of sound mind, I leave all my crayons to . . .

· To my Uncle Ezra, who always said that health was more important than money, I leave my bottle of vitamin C and my torn jogging sneakers.

· To my first husband who always said I never brought him enough excitement . . . I leave my exploding Pinto.

SELECTING AN EPITAPH

Most of us spend more time picking out our scenic checks than we do an epitaph for our tombstone. This is a case of misplaced values. A scenic check is not engraved forever in stone, and a tombstone won't bounce.

What you select for an epitaph says more about you than what you have on your bumper sticker or T-shirt. Don't leave the choice to others. Pick one yourself.

W. C. Fields, of course, had the immortal, "I'd Rather Be in Philadelphia." I can imagine what some others might be planning. Ralph Nader's headstone might say, "Recalled by Manufacturer." Johnny Carson's: "Filling in for Me Tonight Is David Letterman."

I've been thinking about mine. It's a choice between, "Here Lies Phyllis Diller. She Gave Her Body to Science. They Didn't Want It"; or, "Phyllis Diller—She Looks Better Now Than She Ever Has."

You might pick an epitaph based on your occupation or personality quirk. An airline stewardess: "Ocupado." A hotel clerk: "Do Not Disturb." Or, for you hypochondriacs: "See, I TOLD You I Was Sick!"

Good luck.

MONEY MANAGEMENT AND OLD AGE (OR "YOU CAN'T TAKE IT WITH YOU IF IT WON'T CLEAR.")

When I was a little girl my mother told me, "Phyllis, save it any way you can." Then we started talking about money.

I've always linked sex and finance anyway. I guess it's because my dates have always been Standard and Poor.

When you're young and carefree money doesn't seem that important. But to senior citizens, financial security ranks right behind a sober cardiologist as the most important thing they could have. The trick is to invest wisely during your peak earning years.

I personally have not had good luck with my investments. I once dug for oil and struck Teflon. I was a 40 percent owner of a chain of surfboard stores in the middle of Wyoming. I invested in a combination fast-food stand and comedy store called "Joke in the Box." And I don't want to discuss the chain of Phyllis Diller Beauty Parlors. I thought the "exploding hair look" would catch on.

My biggest regret was the Florida deal. A real estate speculator sold me some acres in Florida and convinced me I could retire on the profits. Recently I got bad news and good news. The bad news is a tornado sucked up everything in sight. The good news: It included the guy who sold me the land.

Some people are terrible with money. You may be one of them. You definitely need financial advice if:

- Your grocer won't accept your *cash* without some identification.

- Your bank suddenly announces its new siesta closing hours everytime you walk in.

- You're driving a Desoto . . . and you're still making payments.

For older people on a fixed income it's helpful to keep a budget. I believe strongly in making up charts to see *exactly* where your money is going. With the following money pies you can compare your expenses with others.

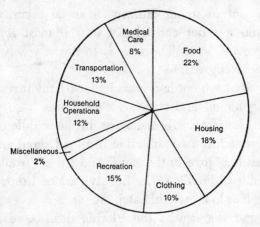

AVERAGE AMERICAN'S EXPENSES

Medical Care 8%
Food 22%
Transportation 13%
Housing 18%
Household Operations 12%
Miscellaneous 2%
Recreation 15%
Clothing 10%

Not everyone has the same budget requirements.

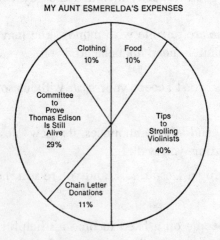

MY AUNT ESMERELDA'S EXPENSES

Clothing 10%
Food 10%
Committee to Prove Thomas Edison Is Still Alive 29%
Tips to Strolling Violinists 40%
Chain Letter Donations 11%

Aunt Esmerelda, of course, was NUTS.

Here is *my* budget . . . to show you what a sane, sensible budget looks like.

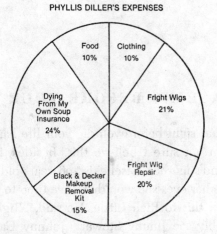

PHYLLIS DILLER'S EXPENSES

Food
10%

Clothing
10%

Dying
From My
Own Soup
Insurance
24%

Fright Wigs
21%

Black & Decker
Makeup
Removal
Kit
15%

Fright Wig
Repair
20%

There! Now that I've taken care of your money worries, let's go to other matters.

SOME THOUGHTS ABOUT SENIOR CITIZENS, DEATH, DYING, THE HEREAFTER AND— SHOULD YOU LOOK YOUR BEST FOR A GLUCOSE TOLERANCE TEST?

Getting shorter isn't the only bad part of getting older. There are other deeper problems. As you get older you start to reflect (when you're wearing Day-Glo orthopedic designer jeans like I do, you *always* reflect), you start to question your values. What is life all about? Have I been a good person? Is it fair that *I* have so much while there may be frightening-looking comediennes in India who are starving?

Here are some other random thoughts from a random mind.

LIFE FLASHING BEFORE YOUR EYES

They say that right before you die your life flashes before your eyes. I'm not sure I believe this. Besides, it's impractical. My friend's mother, Giselle, is 106 years old. If her life flashed before her eyes she wouldn't have time to go.

I mentioned this to Rich Little. He said, "Right before I go, I'll probably see Jimmy Stewart, Johnny Carson, Fred MacMurray, and Humphrey Bogart's life flashing before my eyes."

I've thought it over and I don't want my life flashing before my eyes. First of all, the last thing I need now is another "flash." Also, I haven't had that thrilling a life. I have a feeling that what would flash before me would be the following "lowlights."

1943   GIs voted me Miss Shrapnel Wound.

1946   The year my face and the wine went bad.

1951   Admitted to Beauty Parlor School as a hardship case.

1958   Suspected my husband of messing around. One night as he came home at 2 A.M., I confronted him, "Is there another woman?" I said. He looked at me in curlers, shorty pajamas with bony knees, and face smeared with cold cream and said, "There *must* be!"

1964 Divorced, trying to "get my life together." Into vitamins, exercise, health. Woke up every morning and felt like a twenty-year-old . . . but there was never one around.

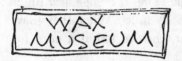

BURT REYNOLDS

1975 Arrested at the Hollywood Wax Museum for turning up the heat and trying to get Burt Reynolds to melt on top of me.

1979 Hollywood premiere of the movie "10." I was not allowed within a five-mile radius.

BODY FREEZING

I've always wanted to be real "cool," but I never wanted it exactly THIS way. The scientific name is cryogenics. Right before you go they freeze your body in ice. When they thaw you out hundreds of years later, they've found a cure for your disease.

I'm not thrilled. All my life my husbands have been telling me I'm frigid. This will confirm it.

REINCARNATION

I'm not sure what this means, but I'd hate to come back as a can of powdered milk.

If I ever do come back in another life, I want no worries and no problems. I want the most comfortable existence in the world. I want to be a poodle in Beverly Hills.

My second choice would be to come back as Miss Teen-age Colorado.

SOME FINAL THOUGHTS

There ARE joys of aging!

In these pages I've put down the aging process and falling faces and creaking bones only because I, like so many of us, are going through it.

It's like jumping on a bicycle without a seat. It hurts as it's happening, but it's also damned funny when you think about it.

Wrinkles, of course, are not the end of the world. They are "love lines" that we women have spent a lifetime earning.

True, it's nice to be twenty-two years old and "Firm." I know it's sad to look back at a high school yearbook and realize that at one time breasts were ABOVE the waist.

But once you've reached your senior years you can find lots of little things to be thankful for.

Be thankful for green grass, grandchildren, and Gable movies on the "Late Show."

Be thankful that cottage cheese, Melba toast, and Sanka are not exported to us by the OPEC nations.

Be thankful that they haven't yet converted Social Security checks to the metric system.

And be thankful that your birthdays are like phonograph records. You were good at thirty-three . . . even better at forty-five . . . and still going around at seventy-eight.